JOB INTERVIEW

Questions and Answers for Your Job Interview
Preparation and Get Hired Fast

(How to Face the Behavioral Interview With
Preparation to Relax and Overcome)

Sherman Metzinger

Published by Zoe Lawson

Sherman Metzinger

All Rights Reserved

Job Interview: Questions and Answers for Your Job Interview Preparation and Get Hired Fast (How to Face the Behavioral Interview With Preparation to Relax and Overcome)

ISBN 978-1-77485-368-9

All rights reserved. No part of this guide may be reproduced in any form without permission in writing from the publisher except in the case of brief quotations embodied in critical articles or reviews.

Legal & Disclaimer

The information contained in this book is not designed to replace or take the place of any form of medicine or professional medical advice. The information in this book has been provided for educational and entertainment purposes only.

The information contained in this book has been compiled from sources deemed reliable, and it is accurate to the best of the Author's knowledge; however, the Author cannot guarantee its accuracy and validity and cannot be held liable for any errors or omissions. Changes are periodically made to this book. You must consult your doctor or get professional medical advice before using any of the suggested remedies, techniques, or information in this book.

Upon using the information contained in this book, you agree to hold harmless the Author from and against any damages, costs, and expenses, including any legal fees potentially resulting from the application of any of the information provided by this guide. This disclaimer applies to any damages or injury caused by the use and application, whether directly or indirectly, of any advice or information presented, whether for breach of contract, tort, negligence, personal injury, criminal intent, or under any other cause of action.

You agree to accept all risks of using the information presented inside this book. You need to consult a professional medical practitioner in order to ensure you are both able and healthy enough to participate in this program.

Table of Contents

INTRODUCTION 1

CHAPTER 1: THE INTERVIEW MINDSET 5

CHAPTER 2: THE PSYCHOLOGY OF INTERVIEWS 24

CHAPTER 3: CARE FOR YOUR RESUME 42

CHAPTER 4: CONDUCTING RESEARCH THE COMPANY AND INTERVIEWERS 48

CHAPTER 5: TAKE CONTROL OF THE INTERVIEW 57

CHAPTER 6: BODY LANGUAGE IN INTERVIEWS INTERVIEW 61

CHAPTER 7: WHAT MOTIVATED YOU TO LEAVE YOUR JOB? JOB? 74

CHAPTER 8: WHAT TO EXPECT AND HOW TO FOLLOW UP 82

CHAPTER 9: SELECT YOUR WORDS CAREFULLY 93

CHAPTER 10: IN THE INTERVIEW 104

CHAPTER 11: THE IMPRESSION FACTOR 117

CHAPTER 12: BRING EXTRA COPIES TO INTERVIEW 130

CHAPTER 13: EXPERIENCES AND EXPERIENCES 140

CHAPTER 14: WHAT ARE YOUR THREE MOST SIGNIFICANT WEAKNESSES? 157

CHAPTER 15: IDENTIFYING POTENTIAL INTERVIEWEES .. 170

CONCLUSION **184**

Introduction

If you're seeking a job and want to impress during a job interview, or a future one then this book is suitable for you. Being successful in a job interview isn't an easy feat, particularly when you're competing with other candidates who are qualified. You need a certain mindset required to masterfully manage a job interview and to be granted the privilege of being hired that is the mentality of salesperson. You represent a company. This company has the name (your company's name) Inc. You are selling your own personal service. You are the top salesperson for the service. Nobody can sell it better than you.

The best salespeople find hidden opportunities to promote their personal service, and they are aware of how to identify the changing market trends and their impact on it. They can tailor the service to suit the requirements of their clients and how to stand out and surpass their competition. The best salespeople are also able to negotiate the cost of their own service in order in order to maximize their earnings/compensation.

This book will teach you how to go from being just a job seeker into a top selling your own personal service. Learn how to become an ideal candidate in employers' eyes and also how to secure the most lucrative compensation for your work.

If you've not thought of yourself as an entrepreneur, I want to remind you that you've been one for all of your life. Your entire existence is a constant communication, persuading and convincing others of your thoughts. Your ability to promote your own personal services to other people will determine the degree of success you have in your work and in your personal life.

A lot of people think that they are salespeople who convinces others to do something that they don't would like to do. They also believe that salespeople are apathetic to other people. The book will help you take advantage of the other. You'll learn to present worth to employers in a manner that will inspire them to choose you.

Being a salesperson for your own service is the act of offering time, consideration and counsel, as well as education empathy, and value. The term "sell" originates in the Old English word "sellan," meaning "to provide."

After transitioning from selling professional into a career coaching I realized I had went from selling services and products to helping others improve their selling and marketing to potential employers. This has given me a unique perspective on the process of interviewing that I offer to you.

There are more than three thousand books on interviewing, However, my book is unique because it's brief, simple concise and to the point. It employs the principles of salespeople who are successful to the job-search process.

The information is designed in a manner which breaks down each step of the interviewing process, starting with the initial interview and ending with the negotiation of salary. It's my absolute pleasure to give you this information.

Chapter 1: The Interview Mindset

The chapter serves as the basis on which chapters to follow are constructed. Although most books devote hundreds of pages of practical guidelines in the last few chapters, they'll be useless if they are not supported by the approach to interview.

What is the reason why the interviewing mindset is crucial? Simply because we embody our beliefs about who that we are. We display our self-declared identity. If you don't view yourself as the best person to be employed then there's no way to play like one.

What is the interviewing attitude? It's a mindset that does not seek anything from anyone and is only for people.

Let me explain.

It's only when you do not seek any kind of attention from others whether it's your attention or affection or their approval. Only when you don't require that can you have the chance to earn it. People are put off by desire, possibly because they are able to see themselves in it. However, when they meet someone who is confident, secure and doesn't needing the public's admiration, they begin to observe.

To complete the deal If this person does not just believe in self-reliance and seeks out the benefit of others, the public cannot help but be drawn to him. Why? Because this seems contrary to common sense. It's not common. If you can learn to master this mentality, you will discover how to win people over.

The truth is that people trust, like and hire those who:

They admire and like

Are interested and like them.

Are they similar to them?

We'll break down this mentality into five fundamentals that are the 5 pillars that form this mentality.

It is essential to build these mental habits over time to get the most out of life's interviews.

Principle #1: You must be the leader.

You can be the leader. When you're not. Be assertive, even if you don't possess the power. In reality, you don't have to be in a post of leadership to convey a sense of authority. Not at all. It's when you present yourself as someone who is aware of what or she is doing. Someone with a solid identity and a sense of purpose.

In the interview In the interview room, this is a sign of are confident in your abilities. It is about going into the interview knowing of knowing that time and energy are precious and important and that you have alternatives (or are likely to have them) and you are aware that the business desperately needs to fill this position and you'll give them time to present the position to you.

When you enter the room with this mindset the way you respond and your attitude will alter. It's going to be totally different when you walk into the room with your fingers crossed and sweaty palms and hoping that people will be impressed by your resume and you from all the 200 other applicants.

No.

It is the first thing to inform yourself that you don't require this job. You'll be able to find other work. You'll discover other avenues. However, your life shouldn't be based on the job you're applying for, or this meeting or the hiring manager. You are refusing to grant the hiring manager power over you.

A military general or CEO would never enter an office, hoping the meeting will go smoothly and that people will be impressed with them. They have a lot of other things to worry of and time precious. Their security, existence and self-worth isn't at risk by anyone in that room, and everyone knows that once they enter.

In this case, you could be tempted to say: They already have work. They already are respected. They're already in that post of leadership, and it's not difficult for them to be respected.

That's why you're not. Since successful CEO's, generals and leaders all had this mentality even before they were ever given their job. In reality it was precisely this attitude that led them to their positions.

All of this is to suggest that you need to get up each day with a clear idea about who you really are as well as what your mission is. If you're not sure of what your purpose is, discover it. Write it down on paper. It is important to understand your role in the world, and what it is that you can contribute that you can only make. You are not Bill Gates, not Steve Jobs Not your boss who is hiring you, and not even your next-door neighbor however, you. What is your unique skill, personality trait or talent that you are unique in that makes you stand out.

Ask yourself What is my speciality? what impact do I have to create?

You may have a keen sense of creating ideas and designs that are yet to be developed, and which the world requires.

You could be an effective organizer and are asked to lead groups of people in new projects.

Whatever the case be, you shouldn't act until you've answered this question.

When you have answered this question and dedicate all of your time to the idea, the process of becoming a leader starts. Once you've embraced this belief system then you'll be able to be able to walk into any space as a leader who has clearly defined goals and personal values. A set of values and a mission that you believe in with absolute conviction are essential and beneficial to the world as well as everyone within it. This includes your hiring manager when you show up to your interview.

Once you've fully accepted this idea of you and your life, you'll begin to transform into an individual who doesn't require any help from anyone else or anything else. This is the start of the journey to leadership.

"The problem isn't about who's willing to allow me in; it's who will block my progress." Ayn Rand.

Principle #2: Be Knowledgeable

"Ipsa Scientia Potestas Est

Knowledge is power in itself."

Sir Francis Bacon

To be a great leader and a true expert in interviews as well as the world it is essential to be well-informed. It is impossible to avoid this. It is imperative to be on an ongoing pursuit of learning and expanding your understanding.

It's easy to identify who the head of this room by observing the people who everyone naturally turn to whenever a question is put to them. Even if they don't hold the authority position in the formal sense. Why? Because they're most likely to be able to answer the question. They're the ones we adhere to.

Every great leader of the past has been a fan of journals, books or magazines, and more recently blogs and online articles. It's only through the habit of reading that you will begin to develop an understanding of how everything is connected in the world. From economics and political science the stock market, human psychology, biology and even chemical reactions.

It's not to say you have to be an expert on all subjects. It would be impossible and would be a waste of time. However, the most effective way to establish the framework for these diverse realms of our lives and societies is to give people access to highest 10% of those who stand out from the rest of the pack. The top 10% of those who are most likely to be monitored.

There's a reason for this.

The reality is that the majority of our education system is flawed because we are pushed to focus on studies over learning. We get rewarded with our test-taking abilities instead of our ability of imagination and achievement.

A majority of the population is taught to follow the rules and to work towards what the system wants to encourage to achieve: A+ grades and study for hours to get through exams (even even if you aren't able to grasp the subject matter) or engage in activities solely to polish your resume, attend the college of your choice and earn an education, learn just for the sake of learning and passing the test, find an internship opportunity or two, and finally begin applying for positions. It is hoped that you will be hired and can begin living your life with ease.

This leads to a society-wide tunnel-vision. We have given up education in exchange for a systematic approach to academics, which is only rewarded when we follow the rules and the structure that has been set on the table for us.

This kind of education is not a way to create leaders.

True leaders go beyond this, whether they do so intentionally or unintentionally, they seek to understand how the world functions. They are interested in learning the ways people interact and how they function.

This is done by way of education and not through academics. It is a personal pursuit motivated by the desire to learn, not by punishment. It is driven by the desire to learn, not by the curriculum.

If you can learn to master the habit of continually studying not just to earn grades and not for the sake of growing and development, then you'll have the chance to make a breakthrough. Few people get through this. A lot of people are content playing the game of academics and do whatever it takes to score good marks or to build a strong resume or to secure mediocre employment and then submit to whatever system, the hiring manager and employers require of them for the duration all their lives.

You have to get rid of this.

When you establish this behavior that you will be a leader , and an individual to follow. You'll strive to be different not just to be conformist. The way you define yourself is your determination to explore the oceans instead of the worry of rocking your boat.

If you can master these two principles that we've been talking about thus far then you'll be someone that people respect and admire and appreciate. This is the first step towards leadership and the first step towards the mindset of interviewing.

Principle #3 3: Make an Affirmation of Expertise

The normal disposition of an individual is to lead a self-centered life. It's a sad fact and, as I stated in the very first pages, it's the way I lived my life.

Human beings tend to be self-centered and self-conscious. It could be called psychology, genetic traits or sin or whatever perspective you are from, we can't deny this fact. However, we can leverage this knowledge to benefit ourselves.

Remember, the three kinds of people people love?

People who they like

People who are a fan.

People who look like them.

The first two rules (be a leader and have aware) will help you become the type of person. People love leaders. People are drawn to those who do not depend on other people. People admire those who are educated.

Being the second kind of human being is the purpose of this concept.

If you wish for someone to love you and trust you, you have to be their most ardent affirmer. You should be their most fervent admirer. You should display genuine interest about their lives and their interests, their experiences, their passions, and even their fears. You should truly desire to learn more about them. They will tell if you're genuine or not.

The only way to truly exhibit border-line obsessional interest in an individual is to present yourself as an individual who does not require any assistance from them. That is to say, let yourself go. It is impossible to be truly interested in their lives in the event that you are completely dependent and in desperate need of their approval or validation.

You should decide with conviction that you don't have to be convinced that this person will like you, no matter if it's a boy or girl you're interested in romantically or even in the case of a hiring manager or a classmate who is new to you. It is essential to locate this sense of self-esteem in other places. You need to feel secure by your own sense of self-worth as well as in your values and in the unique mission you have set for yourself.

Only then, will you be able to dedicate your attention to others. Believe me when I say that such individuals are not common. However, I'm sure you're aware of that.

Let's return into the conference room.

If you go into the interviewing room, don't be anxious about getting the job, because you don't really need this job. Do not wring your hands anxiously hoping that you'll be accepted. Instead when you enter with confidence and conviction and with the belief that you're giving them an opportunity to employ you, you're free to be yourself. You'll be more relaxed and will be a skilled affirmer. The next step is to try to naturally affirm everything it is you could about them, and make them feel valued and appreciated. They'll be able to remember it.

If you are in conversation with strangers whom are the ones you will remember to this day? People who complimented you. People who said nice things about you and also praised your worthiness. Even even if it was as easy as them saying that they liked your shoes or shirt. Do you recall how you instantly were feeling about these people? You loved them.

When you worked as a hiring manager conducting meetings with hundreds candidates in a single day, who would you keep in mind? People who felt affirmed and distinct.

You can say how much you like their outfit, or, when the subject comes up it is possible to casually begin conversations about their interests or even their daily life. Only those who have this approach can achieve this easily and they're the ones who get the chance to become leaders.

Principle #4: Be in Their World

This concept focuses on the kind of person people enjoy: people who have a similarity to them. If you've been to in a new location, whether you've been on the road, or at the start of a new school or even a new job, which person do you prefer to?

People who look like you.

It could be as simple as what they wear and their ethnicity to their personal style and so on. As you meet people better you're drawn more closely to people who have the same interests either in your hobbies, the past, or religion.

People who are in the interview mode are aware of this and will take every effort to create these connections. If these connections are made the hiring manager is 50 percent more likely to recall your name.

Naturally, you'll need to be able to communicate this in a natural way. Also, this doesn't require awkwardly saying, "Hi I'm Henry, What do you like to do?" Experts at this attempt to weave the conversation.

"You've been given a fascinating last name. Can I inquire about where it came from?"

Since everyone loves to talk on themselves, they'll be willing to be sure to. In this case you could say:

"Oh, it's French? I visited France two years ago and it was gorgeous!"

If you did not visit France,

"Oh that's lovely! I have a good friend that's from France who is always talking of _____."

If you're lucky enough, this may bring about a subsequent conversations. It's possible that you won't be in a position to connect easily however, this is an ability you should learn to develop. It is important to learn to train your eyes to look at things that can spark conversations.

What do they say on their coffee mugs?

What is the University Diploma say? What subjects did they take?

What is the meaning behind their tattoos?

If you are able to make an association with them (or anyone else in the world) that will place you in a completely different category all by itself. It will be clear that this ability will be directly boosted in terms of how proficient you are in the fundamentals.

Principle #5: Be Reserved

The fifth and final concept may appear a little off-putting However, there's an important reason behind this aspect of the mindset. It is clear that people admire people who do not display all their cards. I'm not talking about the shady, suspicious sort of way, making people think that you're a criminal.

In reality, I am trying to say to behave so that you're always under control even when you aren't. Always make it appear that you have a different plan to the benefit of other people. Why? Because people look up to those who have answers even if the leaders do not have answers.

This is a normal human trait that is frequently displayed in the films we see. The leaders who are shown to be respected are also depicted as secretive and reserved like they have a secret that we aren't aware of and we should believe them to be right. Some examples include Dumbledore, Professor Xavier, Yoda, Batman, Jack Sparrow, Jesus, Rick Grimes (Walking Dead), Oliver Queen (Arrow). The list goes on and on.

Note that we're borrowing from movies or fantasy. It's more of a reserve. The films simply depict the characteristics of humans. We admire those who appear to always have a clear understanding of what they're doing, and are docile and reserved about it.

Chapter 2: The psychology of Interviews

Interviews are designed to achieve the impossible. They try to dissect a complete human being into measurable, neat traits. The standard questions, the interview cliches - they're used to be there for a reason. Interviewers employ them because they're believed to offer an equal, balanced method to evaluate candidates against one an opponent. Although the answers to these questions provide some clues about the way a candidate is likely to perform on the job, what the interviewer really is trying to figure out is what you're like as a person all. This includes work experiences, critical thinking educational background, as well as the other questions that are asked in those identical, repetitive interview questions you've heard thousand times. However, it also covers factors like your attitude your attitude, your manner of speaking, the impression you create, and how they think you'll be able to get along with your potential team. Thinking about how you can convey all this information in the brief time given in an interview may cause you to spin your mind.

In this section, we'll take an in-depth look at the things that interviewers need to know and how you can show the impression they want. The behavioral and psychological traits that are the basis of a job interview may not be as straightforward as you imagine. There are certain abilities which make the process simpler to master. For starters, the ability to listen and asking the right questions is crucial. This will be covered in the section on Active Listening. Beyond that, the toughest aspect is controlling your nervous system. There are proven strategies that you can employ to ensure that your anxiety doesn't hinder your ability to create the best impression.

What are the things interviewers look for

Interviewers, as we've said in the past, want to see your true personality come through in an interview. This isn't all they require however. They should also ensure that you're competent and try to assess how well you'll fit in with the existing team. It can be an arduous task for an interviewer, however it's good to know that when you'll be presenting at business school, the individuals conducting the interviews are highly skilled and efficient. The following are top fifteen factors that interviewers search at, according to their.

answer the questions. If an interviewer asks you an unanswerable question or with a complex answer it's tempting to turn the question around or ignore it. It's a tactic used by politicians that we've all heard of however the reality is that it can come out as being sly and weaselish. Interviewers will notice that you're not comfortable with the topic If you don't face this question directly, it can make seem like you're indecisive. If this happens, it's generally a query about the weaknesses in the resume or job background. As a result, it's likely that you (the candidate) likely know where the weaknesses are. This is an excellent opportunity to get into! All you have to do is figure out a way to tackle this part of yourself in a manner that's positive, optimistic and truthful. For instance, let's say that you don't have a lot of experience in your work and you've gone straight to graduate school following having completed your undergraduate. It's tempting to avoid answering the question "What experiences do you have to bring to the job." Of obviously, there's numerous ways to answer the question, and bring it back to something you're able to provide a better answer to. It's better and more truthful answer to confront your inexperience head-on. Think of it as, "While I haven't started making my resume I'm planning to tackle the x, y and z issues in the following a, b, and ways." Since you're not trying to dodge something, you're less likely to appear untrustworthy or slippery. After that, you can go on to the next subject which you're sure to have a solid base.

* Ask the right questions. The interviewer will need to know that you've studied the position and, more importantly, that you are aware of the requirements for the position. A quick search on the internet for the company won't suffice to provide the details you require to be prepared to ask questions. Start by reviewing the job description thoroughly. If there are any terms that you aren't understanding or areas you're not more confident in, search at them on the internet. If you're able to ask someone you know from the sector you're applying to and attempt to gain an insider's look at what it takes to be successful. The more you are aware of the job, the more the authority you'll have to communicate with when it comes time to apply.

Find your strengths and match them to the task. Once you have an understanding of the duties of the job think about the abilities you possess that will be suitable for the job. These abilities could be derived from previous experience at work or from your previous life or from your personality. Unless your college distinguishes itself in comparison to other schools of business, then you might decide to leave out some details of your studies you believe will be relevant to the position. The majority of applicants for this job is likely to be a graduate of an identical program and you're better off focus on your unique qualities that separate you from other applicants.

Do some research on the company. It is important to be aware of the company's history but that won't appear, and you shouldn't try to force it. It's far important to be aware of future plans, goals, mergers, or issues that you could be a part of in. Staying up-to-date with company information can help you make inquiries that place you in the position of the business and, consequently an interviewer. This will also give you a live way to put your hiring. This means you will have the ability to identify specific reasons to prove that you are the best person to join the team for any future event.

• Know your goals. Interviewers will try to determine whether your expectations and goals align with what the job and company offer. You'll also need to know the most you can about the possibility of expansion in the job. It's extremely difficult to pinpoint the exact details of this potential ahead of the time. The best approach to deal with the issue is by being sincere, both to yourself and the interviewer about what you're searching for. If you're not happy in a job that has limited opportunities for advancement it's in both your best interests to make this crystal clear. Clearly stating your own self, the things you'd prefer, don't want and should have prior to when you start your job can make this decision much more simple.

• Be ready to display your versatility, resourcefulness, and effectiveness. These traits can be beneficial to anyone in any job however they are essential in the management field. Even if you've only had a few years of working experience to now you ought to be capable of reciting a few stories which show how you've shown these characteristics previously. Be sure that you're comfortable with these tales that you are able to tell them without imposing to engage in conversations. Show a caring and collaborative character. Interviewers will pay particular focus on whether the stories you share and your way of talking show that you are able to be an effective team player or one who is only interested in your own goals. It is important to demonstrate that you are thinking of other people as much as you do. You can show this by your choice of anecdotes as well as by being a good listener and paying attention to anyone you come into contact with during the interview. The interviewer and the secretary who signed your in are colleagues. They'll certainly discuss your experience when you go home, so make sure that you're just as polite with everyone else as you were with the interviewer.

• Be a problem-solver and not a problem-maker. MBA graduates enter interviews with a lot of energy eager to begin their new career and become an inspiration to the businesses who employ them. It can be a disaster if you do not also show a desire to study and fully comprehend all the elements of the problem before you try to tackle the issue. Interviewers often have stories of candidates who tried to showcase their ability to solve problems by offering solutions to companies they're interviewing but failed to meet the criteria. If you're not specifically asked to for a specific story, focus on issues you've solved rather than providing speculative solutions for problems that you might not be able to comprehend in full. If you're ever askedto respond, be sure to base your response by referring to the facts you've learned during your research and interview process. You're trying to display your creative side, but you don't want to be perceived as someone who has jumped to conclusions.

* Respect your colleagues. You're aware that talking bad about your former bosses and your mentors is not a good idea. One of the most common mistakes many make is making their bosses look unprofessional to look better. If the story you tell, meant to show how you've helped save the day, end in making your former boss look like a bunch of scumbags It will result in the opposite effect from what you had in mind. In retelling your story it is often difficult to discern how all of the players are presented to the new set of eyes. While you are able to fill in the gaps in your tale by recalling the details, your audience won't. It's especially helpful to have a colleague and/or advisor hear the story you plan to tell. Make sure that you don't appear arrogant or boastful.

* Take charge of your experience. If you're not blessed with lots of experience in your job, this may seem like a daunting task. If you've been there you've surely had

occasions in your career where you fought through difficulties, improved situations and improved the efficiency of the system you worked. Think creatively about the skills and experiences you possess which demonstrate your capacity to succeed in this role.

Developing Active Listening Skills

Researchers studying communication and listening estimate that we only recall one quarter to half of what people have to say. Consider that for an instant! In reality, we're getting half of the conversation. You'll probably remember a number of incidents in your own life that show this is true. We've all been through the experience of speaking to one person and not feeling like they truly took in what we're speaking about. When you're interviewing the most effective option is to make it clear to your interviewer that this isn't likely to happen when they speak to you. Through active listening will show that you can retain the majority of what's going in the world around you. This shows attention to details as well as empathy and determination to work towards making others feel valued. It is a sign that you are a good manager. Listening actively isn't only useful for an interview for a job, evidently. Every aspect of your life will be enhanced when your listening abilities get more proficient. In this book, however we'll focus on the business aspect that is active listening. The art of listening attentively and mindful listening can be expressed in specific steps.

* Be Present

This is the first one and probably the most difficult. While we're engaged in conversation, the distractions such as responses, rebuttals, and even rebuttals can creep into our brains and take away our ability to concentrate on the person we're talking to. To combat this, we must start before the conversation even begins. Before you step to your meeting, take some time in peace and tranquility in your head. This will not only help you to become more attentive, but it can help you relax. Bring this mindset to your conversations. When interruptions and distractions appear into your head, you can practice making them a prompt to keep your focus. It's not easy initially however, the more you battle the forces that surround you and within your own head and body, the more distracting they'll get. By making your mind work to benefit you rather than to your disadvantage by making them an integral part of your focus process can transform them into a resource instead of a roadblock.

* Acknowledge

A few nods "yeahs," and "uh-huhs" that we use in our conversations may appear to be a bit of filler however, they have a reason. The two issues people often encounter when they first begin to listen are that they do not acknowledge their presence or are hesitant to acknowledge due to fear of expressing an opinion that they aren't completely with. Similar to distractions, these could be transformed into tools for more active listening. In the first scenario you must develop your habit of using each "yeah" or "uh-huh" as a compass which reminds you to listen fully with what a person is speaking to you. It's a process that requires practice but once you've made the connection between these words and attentive listening, it's automatic. Another concern that is a lot more simple to incorporate into your the habit of listening. Instead of using the phrase "mmhmm" or another positive comment Try saying something that expresses clearly your feelings about the conversation. For instance, if someone who you're speaking to mentions something that you're not certain you're with, try by saying "oh fascinating," or "I hadn't thought of this." This indicates that you're curious to learn more, but it doesn't bind your position on the issue.

* Develop Empathy

In addition to being a great life tips, developing empathy can help in improving your listening skills. The easiest way to begin this process (which can last a lifetime in the case of honesty) is to take some time after your interactions with people reflecting on the way they felt about you, how you appeared to them and how you could have handled it better. As time passes you'll be able perform this process in the present without losing concentration.

* Send Feedback

It's not easy to provide feedback without interrupting, however it is possible to do so. One way to cross the line is to rephrase what you're hearing and then checking for clarity. Questions like "So what do you mean by x? refer to that ..." as well as "What I'm hearing sounds like x, is that right?" allow the speaker to elaborate and clarify their meaning when they speak. This means less questions that you have to keep in your mind until the conclusion of the conversation which reduces interjections. It will let them know that you're working hard to grasp every nuance of the words they're using.

* Resist Arguing

If you find yourself tempted to challenge whatever your friend is saying, take it as an opportunity learn more about what they're actually saying. This can serve two functions to ensure that you don't argue with something you don't fully know. Additionally, and perhaps most important in the context of the interview process, it implies that you can reduce the likelihood that you'll be perceived as aggressive and combative. These behaviors are totally unsuited to the image you're trying to portray during an interview. Naturally, there will occur instances where an organization's practices, ethos or its culture is in opposition to your own goals or your morals. In such instances it's best not to get involved because there's no need to destroy bridges.

* Be Patient Before Responding

Even if the argument you're composing isn't an argument, you shouldn't hurry to put it out out there. It's normal to worry that you'll lose the (very crucial) item you're planning on saying, but the reality is that if the topic is crucial, it will be available whenever it's your turn to speak. The best way to transform this distracting urge into a more effective listening tool is to put your own ego aside. While you work on active listening, remember that the aim isn't simply being smart, but actually making progress. It can take some time to establish an habit however the time it will take will save.

It may sound easy, but in reality it's not. The ineffective, poor listening habits we've developed throughout our lives aren't easy to change. Include active listening as a component of your preparation for interviews right from the beginning. When you are thinking of responses to the questions you're expected to answer think about the different ways they could be asked. Consider how your answers should be different with each change. In the weeks, days or even months between this article and an interview for the first time, make an effort to apply these skills and actions to every interaction you are in. When you conduct an interview mock-up in preparation ensure that you are listening actively as the primary focus. Listening skills are just like other skills; the more you utilize it, the more it becomes. Keep in mind that this isn't only about securing a job. The ability to listen can make you more effective as a manager, supervisor as well as an employee.

Chapter 3: Care for Your Resume

Your resume is a representation of you. It is the sole evidence of everything you're capable of having completed your studies at a reputable university. The part that your resume plays in the chances of securing a job is not easily explained into words. Your resume is your image in presenting your self to interviewers. Don't ignore your resume. Make sure you take care of it in just three easy steps.

Step I: Building the Resume

The process of creating your resume should begin when you graduate from school and enroll in a reputable college. From that debate contest you won, to any relay race that you took part in, everything needs to be documented with all the required information, on your resume.

It is crucial to start your career very early. A resume will include all your accomplishments and participations. It doesn't matter which kind of competition you participated in. Your resume doesn't have to be specific in its nature, but it does show how your progress in general. Therefore, it is important to list everything you've accomplished to date.

Keep a diary of your internship. As you work you develop trust and goodwill with businesses and other groups of people that whom you intern under or with. You must ensure that everything you do is documented in your intern diary and, eventually, it will make its way to your resume.

Don't let your vacations go to be a waste. Although they're supposed to be used for the purpose of having fun and fun Don't neglect to dedicate a portion of your time seeking out internships to be at. Have fun but think about the possible opportunities to work and what better time to do that than vacations to improve your resume.

The initial stage of resume is to include high-quality content into it. This can be accomplished by taking part in competitions or presentations. It doesn't matter whether you are a winner or not. Sometimes, just participating earn brownie points.

Step 2 The technicalities of resume

A good resume should include all of your information in a format that is structured. A typical resume contains the following details about the applicant:

Name: Your complete name.

* Your address that is permanent. In general, this address refers to the address you were born or the ancestral home where your ancestors reside.

• Your address at present. The reason you should include your current address is to provide the possibility of easy access to you should the phone number and email address don't work.

* Telephone number (s) together with STD or state code number. If you're selected you will need to make contact. Contacting

them via phone is the most convenient method to do this. Be aware that the phone number you regularly make use of should be made available.

Complete information on your accomplishments. Many times, corporate offices require to verify your claims . Therefore, it's a good idea to give them with all the information needed about the contests you participated in.

The list of your interests is a different area that must be filled in with care. It is typically found at the bottom of resumes in order to give a casual impression to the person applying. However, few people are aware of the significance of this area. For instance, you're looking to join an eminent law firm. If you say that you're interested in family law They will be more likely to offer you a spot in their department of family law.

Another casual area that resumes require you to fill out is called 'Passions'. It is common for people to mention their hobbies. The most effective options include music, reading, poetry, and sports. This section of your resume will let employers know your general persona. Don't leave the space empty as it could suggest that, besides your academics, you are not interested in way of life.

Step III: Fine tuning your resume

Before hitting the 'send button' on the email that includes your resume, review your resume, looking for anyerrors.

A. Problems with the filling up process.

B. Filling in technical slip-ups

C. False or false claims

Be careful when writing something on your resume. It could be that the information you're not writing down isn't really necessary. Write down the most crucial sections first, and then move into the smaller ones. If you can, send your resume to a friend to proofread it.

The final step in creating an effective resume is about ensuring that there is nothing sloppy or misleading about it. It is possible to go through your resume over five times and still discover no flaws. It is always advisable to forward it to a third-party who's in the best position to spot mistakes on your resume.

A great Resume is the single most crucial aspect of your search. Inattention to this can cause you to be rejected and to regret it. A well-maintained and organized resume can be a boon even if you do not have the same qualifications than someone who is more worthy of.

Chapter 4: Conducting Research the Company and Interviewers

Imagine that you're going to an interview for a job that you don't know anything concerning the organization. Do you have a picture of how the interview might go?

If you don't have a lot of knowledge -- or perhaps know nothing at allabout the company you're aiming to join it's likely that you'll look at the interviewer in awe as they are asking you questions like why you're interested in working for the company or what job you envision yourself performing in it.

When you are making a preparation for an interview your first task is collect on all the information you can on the company to prepare your answers and present your case accordingly. Here's what you'll need to prepare for the interview.

Conduct extensive research on the Organization/Company

If you're applying for the job you want, it's important to study the company to know some information about the business that you're applying for and its industry, nature and scope. When you're invited for an interview you'll need to make this research an exhaustive one. Here's what you have to accomplish:

Do extensive research on the company or business online, and learn everything you possibly can regarding its past as well as its work, clientele, its products and services and any challenges that it has had to face, its the past and present achievements and net worth etc. This will allow you to understand its position in the business.

If, for instance, you're submitting an application for a job within a company that's been operating for over 50 years, or a business which is always growing, you'll know you're applying to a reputable business with a lot of growth potential and the motivation to succeed in your job interview will grow.

The successes will give you an idea of the extent of expansion. For setbacks, when you are aware that you possess particular skills or abilities that could help your company overcome a flaw that causes an issue, you can include that information in your pitch to impress interviewers.

In researching the operation and operation of the business, study its products and services to ensure you are aware of what they deal in, as well as the goods or services you'll be working with should you get the job. This can help you think of ways to improve the quality of their products or methods to increase the marketability of their products based on the sector or area of the business that you're interested in working in.

While doing your investigation, make sure to visit the business's website, if they have one. Nowadays, the majority of businesses or organizations have websites, even if it's not attractive. If the business you're applying for has no website, be cautious as it could mean that the business or organization isn't legitimate. But this isn't the case for all businesses that are legitimate. Some firms have local presence but do not have websites. If you can't locate the website, try other sources on the internet for details about the company or the business. Look up any news releases or articles about the business. Also, check LinkedIn for individuals who are associated with the company , or for the company's own profile. LinkedIn is an excellent social media site that can help you meet individuals from the world of business. Additionally, it provides a wealth of information on companies.

Check if the company you're planning to join has a blog. If there is one, examine the details on the organization's activities, its products and services as well as previous or ongoing promotions and deals, achievements and other details that will help you craft an efficient job application.

Visit the company's Facebook or Twitter accounts if they are available.

If it is a public corporation you can check the SEC filings on sec.gov.

Find out about the competition of your company and learn as much as you can on them. This info is useful when interviewers ask questions like how you can assist the business expand or assist in making it better. You could highlight the advantages of your company's competitors and then present your suggestions about how you can help this business succeed by using your talents and skills.

Be sure to print the important information you find through your research. You can then save them in separate folder. You should go through the information several times until you've got an in-depth knowledge of the business or company. If interviewers notice that you have an extensive understanding of the business and its operations, you are sure to make them feel impressed to the level where they will consider you an ideal candidate for that job.

While it is crucial to study the company you're hoping to join It is equally crucial to learn more about the people you interview with.

Find Your Interviewers

If a business or company invites you to an interview, make sure you know the individuals that will interview you. Some businesses prefer to not divulge this information However, in some instances, the person who calls you to set up an interview will inform you of the names of the people you will be interviewing. Be sure to receive both of them from the person to ensure that you thoroughly study the people you'll need to impress during the interview.

Understanding what the people who interview you are essential due to:

It will help you decide the amount of effort you'll need to invest in your preparation. While you must be prepared to give your best effort in every scenario, it's easy to get more focused if you know that the CEO of your firm will be conducting an interview with you.

It can help you investigate the qualifications, achievements net worth, achievements and profile of the interviewers. This research will aid you in understanding what interviewers are seeking in applicants. For example when someone you are interviewing happens to be a web developer with an innovative method of working in the industry , or an entrepreneur with many unique products it is obvious that they will be looking for a person with great imagination and ability to think out of the box. Therefore, in order to impress them your pitch must showcase your talents as creative.

It also allows you to find facts that you can relate to and then convince the interviewer of your qualifications for the position. For example, if a particular interviewer has one million dollars in net worth however, he started out from scratch six months ago, you could make your pitch that describes the hard work, determination and perseverance.

You can also learn about the preferences, interests and dislikes of the interviewers, and then make use of this information to draw their attention. For example, if you are aware that an interviewer is a golfer and you want to discuss the sport (at the right time) to impress him or her.

The main objective is to get a better understanding of the interviewers' background and professional profiles as well as their interests so you can build a good relations. To do this follow these steps:

Conduct online research about each individual

Look up profiles of individuals Explore profiles of individuals on Facebook, Twitter, Instagram, LinkedIn, and any other social media platform to learn more about the interests, likes, dislikes and interests, accomplishments and more.

Check out the information you have about your interviewers on the website of the organization.

Gather as much information as you can about both the company as well as the interviewers. Make a softcopy as well as a hardcopy of your information so you can read it when you don't have an internet connection or laptop.

After you've done your research about the interviewers and the company The next step is to prepare yourself for frequently asked questions, so that you can respond effectively.

Chapter 5: Take Control of The Interview

Many who are selected to an interview are filled with hopes, but when they don't get a call back following an interview might be extremely disappointed as this implies that they'll be to look for jobs again. This is why the little effort to ensure the success of your interview is so important. You must be prepared to impress your interviewer and in order to ensure that you're getting the job you want in the final.

Making sure you are in control of the interview is one of the ways by that you can be sure of that you are successful at the conclusion of the interview. You're looking to have a bit of excitement and optimism after the interview. And after a few days or in the same manner you'd like to get the positive news that you have been offered the job. Here are some strategies that can help you achieve excellent results in the final:

Learn what you are trying to accomplish in the interview

Most job seekers do not understand the role they play in an interview. Most people think they're in the interview is to inquire for a job. However, their role is much more than that. The most important thing you need to do by the end of your interview process is prove to the panel of interviewers that you're the best person for this job. another is to figure out whether the opening for the job is the type of job that you've always been interested in.

Talk

Many experts will advise that you should be a story-teller in an interview. Although this might not be the case for all interviewees, especially those who tend to be anxious but it could work to your advantage and increase your likelihood of being selected for the job. Interviews are supposed to be something like an exchange between two or more people so you should be able tell your story in a captivating and professional way. This is why taking the time to perfect the art of storytelling is an essential part of your preparation. Don't leave the questions to the interviewer on its own and you must create your own questions in order to keep the interview interesting and ensure that you've taken control of the interview at the time you finish the interview.

Do not get emotional

If you have emotions that you're struggling with, try to make sure to keep them away from the interview during the time of your interview if it is important for you to achieve success. Interviewers can provoke interviewees into being emotional. If you're still carrying your baggage return to the interview there is a chance that you'll become emotional, and it can become out of control. This isn't best for your health. You must show your potential employer that you are able to handle any stress and emotion that it happens and not let it overtake you. This is what makes someone perfect suitable for this job.

Do not ask for an opportunity to work

Some job seekers appear to be desperate and that reduces their chances of being hired even if they're fully competent for the job. If you wish for yourself to remain on the safer side, don't beg to be hired. The essentials to live a full life, such as water and air but you don't require to be employed. Make sure you show your prospective employer that you're ready and ready to provide solutions for their business. Employers should know that employers will not select you because of sympathy but because they believe you're the best candidate to be hired. If the job isn't yours, you must move on quickly.

Chapter 6: Body language in Interviews Interview

While your interview answers are vital the lack of or improper body language could reduce your chances of securing an interview and could be a reason that you won't be accepted. Effective ways to communicate include eye contact, smiling and solid posture, as well as active listening and the occasional nod. Unpleasant ways of communicating with your body include slouching and looking at the distant or playing with a pen and fidgeting on chairs, rubbing the hair back, or touching the face when talking or making a mumble.

Your resume is crucial and so are your communication and social abilities, but don't undervalue the significance of body language during the interview process. Be aware that your body's posture should convince anyone looking at you that you're at ease and confident. When sitting, make sure you resist the urge to slump your shoulders and put your chin in your chest. Such gestures can cause you to appear uneasy about your own self and close off. Make sure you sit on your stomach with your spine straight, and with your shoulders wide. This will help you appear more professional and in control of your feelings, which will consequently look professional.

Your body language tells an awful lot about you as an employee who is a candidate and could sabotage your chances even before you know what's happening. The confident people display a different body language. They are in a straight line. They don't let their heads drop. They stare at the eyes of other people. Also, they keep their bodies wide.

When we are feeling down in our self-esteem, or are hurt or down and we are prone to shutting down. Not only physically but also emotionally. We strive to be as small and positive as possible so that others aren't aware of us. Our bodies are curled, which means we reduce the area of our exposure.

Insecurity manifests through body language. A method to boost confidence is to use a body language that indicates someone who is confident. It's a fact that being late could make you appear unprofessional and reduce your chances of being hired, but getting there early may transmit a negative impression. For instance, arriving 30 minutes early to the interview does not appear responsible; it just makes you look awful and in some cases even in desperate situations. A five-minute delay is ideal, it will make you appear competent, but not overly eager. It is crucial to time your arrival Keep that in your mind.

Additionally the posture of having an upright back and your chest open can be seen as a clear indication that you're confident about your capabilities and abilities and also that you are an assertive person. But, do not add the impression of being aggressive. There's a clear line between confidence and intimidation. A confident candidate is able to get the job however an intimidating candidate doesn't. Perhaps he is when the job is one of a bouncer at a nightclub. In other jobs, avoid this kind of behavior.

Additionally, it is important to know that interviewers decide to hire within the first 5-10 seconds of meeting the applicant. The way you enter the room plays a role in of that judgement. Be sure to walk straight towards the interviewers you're talking to, with your body pointed towards them, keeping eye contact, with occasional breaks in the direction of the other.

When you are making eye contact, be careful not to take it too far. One way to keep your eyes at the camera and be engaged is to examine various parts of the face of the interviewer which includes the nose, eyes mouth, lips, forehead and then look into the eyes of the interviewer. During the interview, be sure that you expose your palms. When your palms are exposed they signal the honesty, kindness and commitment. This gives off a positive vibe and make the person you interview relaxed. Also, open palms, coupled with a good posture makes your appearance more lively and confident.

It is equally important to pay attention to your breath. It is an extremely important element of an interview. The most effective method is to breathe in during the time when an interviewer is asking you questions and then answer when you exhale, taking in the flow of air.

If everything went smoothly, don't down, do not relax. When you are done with the interview, put down your time, stand slowly, smile and shake your head. If handshakes with the other people in the room isn't comfortable, be sure to at the very least meet the manager before leaving the building. Do not begin analyzing how you performed during the interview while in the building. the people around you will notice and could consider it to be a sign of an indication of insecurity. Take a moment or two, and then do it in a place where nobody are able to observe you.

Phone Interview

In recent years interviews conducted by phone have become more frequent. They're extremely useful because they can save lots of time and also the elimination process is completed in much less time. In essence, telephone interviews and interviews conducted on Skype are very like in-person interviews. Interviews are typically performed by hiring managers and recruiters as a helpful instrument for screening applicants for the position. Since 2005, a growing amount of businesses began the interview process via a telephone call or Skype in order to talk about the job opening with potential employees to determine if the applicant is suitable to the job.

Businesses conduct phone interviews for a single reason. It's a wonderful method to find and select potential candidates for jobs. It's a time-saving as well as efficient method of conducting interviews, particularly in the initial and often second round of the process of elimination. Interviews conducted through Skype can also be used as the best way to cut down the cost of the process of selection.

The majority of the time interviews are scheduled several days or weeks ahead. However, you shouldn't be apathetic as there's always the possibility that you'll receive a surprise phone call.

There's no way to know the moment that a prospective employer or network contact may call to inquire if you are available for just a few minutes to chat to them. Always be prepared to answer the phone professional, particularly when the number is unidentified. It's true that the phone and Skype interviews pose particular difficulties. It is essential to be as prepared as you would for any other type of interview because an interview over the phone could be the only opportunity to impress on the representative of your prospective employer.

According to the old saying that you will never have another opportunity to make a good first impression. Be sure you're completely prepared for the interview, as a phone call does not give you the opportunity to revise your ideas.

The best way to prepare would be to prepare as prepared as you possibly can for the interview. Prepare yourself to answer any questions that might be asked and research the company , and know the answers to any question the manager who is hiring you. Examine these questions and their responses, and you'll dramatically increase your chances. The practice is not just going to make you appear stronger, however it could be able to help you identify that you may have some language issues that could be distracting or if there is a an inclination to speak too slowly or too quickly.

When you practice answering questions, ensure that you record the practice. After you have heard the recording, you'll have a good idea of what your voice is like over the phone. If you notice on the recording that you tend be prone to making "uhm" sound or stutter slightly when you're anxious, you can take a deliberate effort to correct it.

If you're invited to an interview by telephone or Skype interview, take a look at the most common questions you'll be asked. Don't forget to make the list of questions for the person you interview. This can help you find lots of information about the company that could provide you with a clearer picture of the position you're looking for, and it can also make you appear professional. A majority of top candidates are keen to learn more about what it's like to work for the business, and also what will be their chances of advancement at the firm, in the event that they were offered the job.

Do not undervalue how important it is to have a telephone interview. an effective phone interview can be your chance to move on to the next phase in the process of hiring, and the negative impression could cost you with no chance to make yourself known in the best light. Most of the time, phone interviews aren't so as much conducted with the intention of securing employees, but are designed to rapidly get rid of candidates who aren't deemed to be a suitable fit for the prospective employer.

After the interview has begun, you should be sure to follow the guidelines that will improve the chances of success interview via phone or Skype interview:

1. Keep your resume handy for you when you are interviewing.

So you'll be able to review it when you have to answer questions about your previous experience at work.

2. Create a list of your skills that meet the criteria for hiring.

Prepare the list prior to the interview and be prepared to discuss how the qualifications meet the requirements. Keep the list handy so you are able to look it up when you are in the telephone interview. It is advisable to emphasize the most important qualities needed required for the job and highlight them when you are offered the chance.

3. Make sure that the space is not occupied.

The last thing you need is screaming children or barking at your dog while you are interviewing. It could cause you to lose your focus and make you look very inept. Think about the question: would you choose to hire someone whose children or dogs bark as they're interviewing them? I doubt it.

4. Focus on the interview. It is crucial to concentrate your attention on what you are doing during the interview.

Make sure you take the time to listen carefully to the question and politely ask to clarify your question if not certain what the interviewer wants to know. If it's your turn to respond, do so slow and clearly. Do not feel pressured to respond immediately. It's perfectly acceptable to give yourself a few moments to think before responding.

5. Do not disrupt the interviewee.

If you aren't happy with the way they're talking about or are uncertain about the question you're asked, don't interrupt. You'll have the opportunity to request clarification.

6. Take a walk about the area.

Let's do something. You can talk while sitting in a chair with your body is in a slump. You don't sound energetic are you? Then, take a walk around the room while you're talking via the phone. Choose a pace you're comfortable with. If you're walking faster, you'll project more energy as well as the other interviewer sense it, whether consciously or subconsciously. If you sound this way, you sound competent and confident, and that is the impression you'd like to leave on the interview.

7. Smile throughout the conversation.

Make sure to smile. A smile can convey an image of positivity to the person listening (in this case, the interviewer) and can alter the sound of your voice. If you're uncomfortable moving around during your interview, sit when you're speaking. The standing position also gives your vocalist more enthusiasm and energy.

In preparation for the questions of an interview, be sure to answer questions you believe are relevant for the job. The questions should generally relate to your prospective duties and roles at the company. It's only natural that you're eager to understand what you'd perform if you got the job. Of course, you'll need to be aware of the scope of your responsibilities should you be selected. Inquiring about these types of issues will help you appear more professional and active. In addition, it can make you stand out from the other applicants since the majority of potential employees do not have questions during an interview.

Chapter 7: What Motivated You to Leave Your Job? Job?

This type of question typically makes many interviewees nervous. There are two main reasons why you quit an employment position: willingly or unintentionally. If the former is the case that you quit the job in a voluntary manner, but you'll need to clearly explain the reason you left. For example, explain to them why you've been looking for a different task.

In the case where, for the second time when you've been dismissed, it's best to admit it. It's important to share with them what you have learned from the experience, and the steps you took to address the reason for being fired.

When you ask this query, there are three things that your interviewer will want to learn about you:

Did you quit your job because of the right motives?

The person you interview with would be interested in knowing whether you're solid, reliable, accountable and reliable. (S)he might also wish to assess your values at work:

Do you feel you were not appreciated or undervalued in your previous job?

If you believed that you had achieved everything you set out to do within the company, or was it because of your exaggerated feelings of being important?

Did your ego, or your abilities exceed your accountability?

Have you been asked to leave or did you leave by yourself?

If you were told to leave, and why:

Did you encounter any integrity or performance-related issues?

Did that happen because of other factors like mergers, downsizing, etc. ?

If, for instance, you quit your job by yourself, the interviewer would be interested in knowing whether it was legitimately a reason for leaving.

Did you depart with the professional look?

Are you still on good relations with your previous company? Your former employer might serve as one of your references if you quit as a professional.

These are a few methods that your interviewer might employ to determine whether or not you're an accountable employee because you have the qualities that correspond with the standards and values that the company is looking for.

Common Faults

The specifics of the answer you provide in this query are likely to be discoverable (i.e. confirmable). Therefore, you should be cautious not to be caught up in trying to erase your past.

Never lie about your prior position(s)

It's possible that the Interviewer and the former supervisor might know each other or are connected in any way. Many industries are in fact smaller groups than one might otherwise think of. Therefore, in the event where you're confronted with this type of question, make sure to be honest and direct The interviewer might already have the answer!

No trash-talking former employers

There are only two possibilities for why someone would make the decision (ahead of the time limit or at the present) that it's okay to criticize about a former employer. One, you're still angry about your former job and you can't resist the urge to be a victim of that bitterness. It may also feel somehow empowering to take on the role of judging the motivations or motives that led to your decision to terminate. However, for any reason you can imagine what the interviewer might be listening to: "Someday, if you terminate me, I'm sure to have to slander you and the firm!" It's not worth the risk! Respect the interviewer and adhere on to your facts.

Don't be a job-changer

Do not say you're looking for an opportunity to make a change due to being bored of doing the same thing. You may have felt that you're in the right place to change your profession, and you'd rather test your skills at the position they're offering. It is essential to provide an argument that proves you're the perfect candidate for the position.

Answering the Question : What made you leave your previous job?

The more you attempt to come up with an answer (prior to interview) the greater the odds of making it sound perfect!

Remember that the main thing to remember in this case is to make your answer concise, positive and clear.

In contrast to other questions, that are based on the need to throw the ball in a curve and see your reaction, this one is more likely to let you know the reason you're on a job hunt. This means that you should make use of it as an opportunity to prove to your interviewer why you are the ideal candidate for this job.

If you have left without hesitation...

If you have left your previous firm with a positive attitude, then you should prepare an exact example of a talent, ability, colleague, another characteristic that you like and that your company has. This is beneficial by two different ways. In the first, you're providing an intelligent, positive motive for leaving your former employer and something they would not have been able to give. In addition, you're likely to praise the prospective employer by highlighting a worth that they have over their competitors.

If you've been terminated ...

If you've been dismissed, be honest and explain the reasons for your dismissal and take responsibility for the incident. Be clear about the lessons you have gained from the incident, and also the factors led to the decision. The interviewer will be aware human error however they will be interested in knowing what steps you took to address the reason of your termination.

Pro Tip: Avoiding the possibility of termination

Do not hesitate to use phrases like 'budget cuts' or downsizing if they are real and they are the primary reason for quitting the company. Don't overstate circumstances however to the extent that you can minimize your mistakes as causal reasons for your dismissal then all the better.

Chapter 8: What to Expect and How to Follow Up

Do not be afraid to inquire regarding the progress of your interview. In the end, it's appropriate to find out if you're still in the hunt for the position or if they've made a decision to take you off the list. Be aware that the quicker you find out about the decision of the company and the quicker you'll be able to progress in your career projects. This will bring you closer to the most appropriate job faster.

Apart from making your life more quickly, doing following-up with your contacts can help you stand out from the throng of applicants for the job you are interested in. The hiring manager might be impressed by your enthusiasm for the job. This is also an opportunity for you to refresh your professional and positive impression you made in the initial interview. If you feel that you've left other impressions with the person who is hiring you Following up on the interview could make a difference.

To make sure that your follow-up efforts are beneficial for you by keeping the following points in mind while making plans and carrying out post-interview tasks.

Make sure you follow-up on both your face-to face and telephone interviews to confirm you've succeeded to find an employment.

It is the quickest and most convenient method of communication. But written notes or letters that are handwritten can be more individual and thoughtful. You could choose based on the impression you wish to leave with your employer.

Make sure you follow up with the appropriate person. Do not continually nag or harass the assistant of the hiring manager or the receptionist on the situation regarding your appointment. It's likely that they're ignorant as, or more ignorant than you are about this aspect.

Utilize emails, letters or notes to reaffirm that you are interested in the job which you've been able to interview for.

Timing is crucial to. The idea of sending an email every hour or even daily can be a hassle to a busy person. Give yourself at least a week before sending the first message. After that, spread your follow-up attempts by at least three days so that the development can occur.

Make sure you say it correctly. Make sure to proofread your email or letter prior to sending it out to ensure that they are free of spelling and grammatical mistakes. A short introduction spiel and practicing it prior to the actual call may aid in easing the tension and also lessen the excitement.

Don't think you're in the way of a potential employer when you follow up after an interview, especially first time. Some employers give you a period of 2 to 3 weeks before ending a job offer to determine who will follow-up to demonstrate their interest.

Also, don't be a victim of anything. Some people might not be capable of accommodating you every day, so be flexible. If you ever don't get selected for the position - keep it! Be grateful and polite to demonstrate that you're an actual winner. This will help you build a reputation or networks that can be beneficial for the future.

If You've Made It Past The First Round

You're among the fortunate ones , my dear friends. Of course , the successful first job interview isn't just based on luck. It is based it is based on months and even decades of work. Successfully completing your first interview does not mean you are able to take a break and not be concerned. As you're an inch closer to securing the job, preparing for your second chance should encourage you to be prepared and present yourself more effectively. The saying goes second chances don't come often. Don't waste them by displaying excessive confidence.

Conducting the second interview exactly as the first interview might be unwise. Although many aspects might be the same however, there are some differences to be expected and appreciated at the second stage of hiring. Dress code, grooming and pre-requisitions are the same, unless stated contrary. Expect to interact with more people who work for the company or applicants for the position. Be prepared for the possibility of increasing competition and challenges to this stage to succeed in this phase.

Follow these suggestions to increase your chance of getting hired in the second interview.

Include the names of people you've spoken to during your previous interview, when greeting them. A person who is flattering in this manner will earn you brownie points for this particular level.

If you are required to confirm your attendance, do so to demonstrate your interest in the job. You might also inquire about the things that are required or expected of you on the day. If they are willing then ask about the method of the interview to be held.

Take a look at your notes previously made regarding the company. Learning details about the company, its customers and the work they perform among others will show that you're interested and concerned about their business and help you get closer to the end of the road.

Learn more about the position you're applying for by studying the industry norms, such as the job description and salary in order to effectively negotiate if necessary.

Do a mock meeting with the family members and acquaintances to help you avoid mental blocks.

You'll be more confident this time. Feel proud of the fact that you successful in your first interview. Believing that you are too harsh on yourself following such a feat is not acceptable. Do not forget to have fun and enjoy the process of exploring new areas.

The next time do not just respond to questions. Interview them as well. Being asked for a subsequent interview can be a excellent opportunity to answer any questions that you've had following the first. Additionally, it is suitable to inquire about company the policies and procedures of the company to determine if you're comfortable with these. Make use of this time to meet the employees and the company more.

There is a chance that you will be rewarded with an offer to work after the interview, but don't be rushed. Make sure you are honest about whether you require an extra moment to consider the offer due to other opportunities or other factors. If you don't have any objections regarding the job or company and you are able to accept the offer immediately is fine.

Accepting the Job or Politely Rejecting

Congratulations! The prize for winning has been given to you. It is now the opportunity to feel proud in beating out other applicants and getting the job. As you mentioned said in my introduction you're just one step closer to realizing your goals, responsibilities goals, hopes and dreams with this role. I'm sure you're feeling the pressure of deciding to accept the position right then and there. The reality is that what you've endured isn't an easy task. It's time to say goodbye to attending a variety of interviews and going through endless preparations every chance you're given.

It's not a fast Roadrunner. Keep your horse in check and allow plenty of time to consider these issues before making the final choice of accepting or declining your job proposal.

1.The company: At this point, it's not necessary to spend your entire life in that specific business. However, you must ensure that you are at ease enough with the company to last at least one year. Check to see if are comfortable in the office as well as the possible co-workers, policies, the size, location and financial requirements, among others. Be sure you're willing to accept the mission, values and goals of the business prior to accepting the offer in order to avoid tension and discontent in the near future.

2.The job: It is recommended to consider whether you're capable of completing the tasks the job demands of you. If there are specific skills or requirements that you're not sure of How do you prepare to master these or increase the learning curve. Understanding the hours of work required by you each week is another important factor to consider.

3.Opportunities to learn and grow There is no one who wants to remain stuck and stuck in one place for long periods of time. Before you accept the job offer, speak with the manager in charge of hiring about salaries as well as allowances, benefits, incentives and leave, as well as tuition assistance programs in the event that you choose to pursue postgraduate studies or refresh your knowledge with trainings and seminars that could be offered both inside and outside in the United States. It is also advisable to become familiar with the structure of the company for more information about promotions options within the organization.

Accepting a job offer can be more straightforward than refusing it. Some people may think it's crazy you turn down an opportunity to work, especially in the case of an established company. It's not that difficult and could even benefit you in the end. If you believe or think that you will not be able to support the business with all of your heart, don't be afraid to give it up. When you do this you're not just doing yourself a favor but also your company.

Be grateful for the opportunity, time and the chance that your company has offered you even for a brief period of time. Be courteous is the standard. It's possible to decline the offer, but you should keep the relationships you've formed during the process. You'll never know when the networks can benefit you.

Chapter 9: Select Your Words Carefully

A lot of people are denied chances because they don't utilize the correct and professional language in an interview. If you are not using the correct grammar in your daily life, you'll need to do so during an interview. It might seem acceptable to make use of double negatives and slang when have to deal with your friends or colleagues, but if you need to impress your interviewers in an interview, you should behave as if you have been educated.

In an interview, do not in any way, employ the words slang or curse. For some, this might be a matter of thinking about your words before you speak but it's essential requirement if you are hoping to land your dream job or an opportunity to get a new one. What is acceptable in your current workplace or your home isn't acceptable during an interview. The words you choose to use can affect the likelihood of being selected for the position for which you submitted your application. If you're not confident about your grammar skills, invest some time to study the most commonly used words before going to an interview.

The subject of your conversation is another place that you must remain professional throughout an interview. Even if the person who you interview it is not advisable to use the interview to discuss stories or other information that is not related to the subject of the interview. There's a place for personal conversations and the job interview isn't one of them. Make sure you choose your words wisely and ensure that they relate to the interview, and ensure that you portray yourself as an expert rather than someone seeking more education. Do not use words with meanings you don't know to make yourself appear like you're smarter than you really are. If you make use of a word in the wrong context, you'll look desperate and make yourself appear more attractive to the interviewer. It could result in you losing the job for that position for which you're applying.

Multiple Requests: Selecting the best option

What can what do you decide to do when have to send out numerous resumes and receive multiple inquiries for interviews? If you're unemployed, the time constraint isn't a problem but what happens when are looking for a job change but have only the time to attend interviews? What should you pick the numerous requests? The best thing to do is to select the ones that match the type of job you're looking for. If you are given a short time frame, it's crucial to pick the interview that will help your career the most.

If you're looking at a number of possibilities that could make good job options, you'll have to consider all possibilities, including taking a couple of hours off from your current job to attend the interview that is most appealing to you. If you limit yourself to a specific number of interviews, then you might have a difficult time finding the job you've always wanted. This doesn't mean that you have to devote a significant amount of time away from your present job to attend each interview for a variety of jobs. But you should be able schedule your time in order that you are able to attend every interview you enjoy the most. Be wary of accepting interviews that don't specifically promote your selection of career.

When you've been capable of managing your time to accommodate interviews for the jobs which best fit your career goals You must be sure to follow the correct procedure for interviews to improve the chances of being selected. So, you should dress professionally and have an appropriate conversation during the interview. If you narrow down the choices of interview opportunities you'll be able to handle everything without affecting your work schedule or responsibilities. Make sure you are selective, but make the most suitable career options simultaneously to reduce the length of your interview.

Interviewing Multiple People

Certain companies may opt to conduct an interview with more than one applicant simultaneously instead of 2 separate interview sessions. This will save time for the applicants and them. It is an excellent opportunity for the department head to ensure that all of them can gather and ask questions about the applicant simultaneously. It also helps the candidate from having to attend another interview if they're qualified for the job. It will be simple to Human Resources to review the qualifications of each applicant and identify the applicants who most closely match the needs that the organization needs. Interviewing more than one interviewer will provide the applicant an opportunity to ask questions, without repeating the same questions like when applicants have a one-on-one meeting with every person who is part of the hiring process.

Interviews that involve more than one interviewer successful? Are applicants able to conduct interviews with each individual in a separate manner? If the applicant is having to leave work to sit for an interview, they will save time by meeting the entire group of key decision makers at the same time. This will also reduce time for the company since they will not need to schedule numerous interviews with various people at with different dates. This will also reduce the duration of the process for selection because the normal process of two or three steps now is reduced to just one.

This kind of interview is suitable for both large and small businesses, though larger companies are more likely to utilize such a method to interview. The type of interview could be stressful or uncomfortable for some applicants. They must take into account that they will have to meet with the same participants at some point during the process of interviewing, however it will be more efficient and better than having a meeting together with Human Resources, asked to remain longer or return for a different time to speak with the department heads who will actually make the final decision. In the overall plan of things, it's simpler to talk to all of them at once rather than having to come back or stay for longer than you originally planned.

The Keys to the Success of an Interview

An interview that is successful does more than simply being presentable and proving to the interviewer that you have the appropriate qualifications to be hired. This doesn't guarantee that you'll be selected for the position. The first step to getting selected is convincing the interviewer. That means that you must prove the depth of your expertise. Don't be too confident. Even the most skilled candidate could be denied a job due to they had poor interviewing abilities.

One of the most costly mistakes one can commit is to apply for jobs for which they're not qualified. They attempt to convince the interviewer that they're qualified to do the job. Even if you believe you have the best training on the planet If a company states they require someone with prior experience it is best to possess the necessary knowledge or master it quickly.

Whatever your qualifications are, If you don't present an image that is professional, you are not likely to be hired. A majority of youngsters don't realize this as they don't follow the advice of others regarding the proper attire for interviews. The issue is that , if this is their first job, they may not own any other clothing however, if you are hoping to get hired, you have to purchase appropriate attire for your interview. Many restaurants and retail outlets might not care, but some other businesses may decline your application due to your attire in an interview. Professionally dressed or at least formal attire and be at the right time. If you're likely to be late due to of circumstances outside your control, contact and inform the interviewer of your situation and offer them the choice of seeing you later or rescheduling your interview.

Preparation

Even if you're going to take a job interview There are some steps you can take to prepare for your interview. If you're looking for an opportunity to change your career, particularly one that could result in the possibility of a raise in your salary or benefits, you must impress your potential employer. If you're coming from an interview that was more casual, be sure you're wearing clothes that conform to the dress code of the company with which you're going to interview with.

Even if you've sent or faxed the resume you have submitted, it's an excellent idea to carry an original copy along with you. Interviewers often inquire about the details on your resume and it's much simpler for you to answer if you carry an official duplicate of your resume with you. Don't attempt to recall everything in your resume, particularly in the case of a long professional history. In the event that you are unable to remember the dates and events listed on your resume can look inexperienced and unprepared for an interview. In the majority of cases most interviewers require an updated version of your resume since they typically took all sorts of notes on the resume that you've previously handed in and want a new copy to read at the time of interview.

It is important to pick your outfit the night prior to the interview to ensure you can take the time to ensure you're dressed appropriately and press any items that might be wrinkled. Be cautious about the color you pick - choosing bright colors can distract your attention. Make sure to stick with solid dark shades and select clothes that are conservative and not too flashy. While this is more applicable to women than to men however, it's an important point worth making. The interviewer should focus on you, not at your cleavage.

Keep a notebook with a pen for notes. There will be certain details that you'll need to keep in mind to refer to later on, like working hours, regulations and rules and most importantly, the name of the interviewer to be able to send an "thank for the opportunity" note.

Chapter 10: In The Interview

The Basics

Now , we are getting ready for the interview. We've prepared for the interview and we've gone over the most frequently asked questions and have conducted some practice interviews too. We're aware of everything about the company, their competitors and the rest of the important details that we must know. we're prepared to begin.

Now all we have to do is to look over some things that may appear common sense, but are nonetheless mistakes people make due to the fact that they didn't think about it or were unsure if that it made a impact. Whatever the reason take note of these tips to ensure you give the best impression possible.

Remember to be on time

You're seeking someone who can offer you an opportunity to work. The job will require you to be expected to keep your word and be punctual every single day , unless have a valid reason to be late. Don't begin your day with an unflattering note by not showing up at the right time to your interview. If you do not have a compelling reason for it, and it is made clear to the appropriate people in advance it could put you out of the race.

Take extra time and consider traffic consideration along with the weather. You should arrive within a half-hour before the interview. You could always stay in the car and relax and read your book or grab an espresso. However, you must get to where you're supposed by 15 mins earlier prepared and ready to go.

Be Good

Contrary to what some believe good people tend to do better than rude or sour people. People who are able to get together with other people are usually more popular than the entitled, obnoxious self-centered type of person.

Demeanor and personality are two aspects which are extremely important when it comes to an interview. The person interviewing you will look for evidence that you're competent enough to be able to complete the task, and also that you are nice enough to blend well with your colleagues. If you fall short in any area and you'll likely not get the job.

Look Nice

I understand that the appearance of a person is only from the outside and does not necessarily reflect the type people you're the level of an employee you are. However, how you present yourself is crucial to the first impression people get of you. A lot of times, they look at you prior to speaking to you. Therefore, it's important to present yourself in the manner that those who work in your field are expecting you to look.

If you're having a problem about people judging you based on your appearance, you're entitled to the right to feel this way and how you'd like. But , as we've already stated, it is your responsibility to impress them and not to force them to believe what you wish to be accepted. The choice is yours and solely yours.

However, if you are determined to attend the financial planner's interview wearing 14 facial studs, four nose rings together with the hair that is purple and 74 tattoos, don't feel disappointed when you don't get the job. There are decisions to be made, and we are liable for the results of our decisions.

An appropriate dress code could be formal or casual, based on the job interview and post. Personally, I would advise men to wear an appropriate suit or at the very minimum a tie and jacket and women to dress in a classy dress. This applies regardless of the job you're applying for. Dressing appropriately indicates respect for the employer and the interviewer , as and a commitment to the job.

Be Courteous

You must be polite throughout your life, and especially with those whom you interact with during your interview. When I say everyone, I'm talking about every single person. Certain companies make you wait for a long time and then ask the receptionist to tell you how you were you were waiting. Did you take your time waiting or do you sound annoyed and look at the clock. At times, every aspect of your visit from the moment you arrive to the moment you step out is recorded and written for a specific reason.

Be positive

Interviewers LOVE positive people. You should spend the interview making all positive comments. Let them know what you can accomplish and what you've accomplished. Don't spend time explaining the things you aren't able to do or saying negative things about them. If they ask you to talk about something negative, do your best to change it into something positive by the end of the response.

Learn from your mistakes and hopefully you have examples of how making mistakes can help you improve for the next time. Eliminate negative phrases and words and make your life as positive as you can. Nearly everyone enjoys positive people more that negative individuals. This includes colleagues too, and that's why it matters to a great extent.

Be confident and strong

Interviewers are attracted to those who are confident about their own identity and their talents and skills. They are looking for individuals who aren't too hesitant to take a decision or express their opinions. They don't want someone too smug to act unless they have they are able to get approval beforehand.

The most effective people in the world are those who don't hesitate to take action fast when they are aware of what the best option is. Undecidedness costs time and money , and could be a cause of missed opportunities, and dissatisfaction with customers.

Remember, however interviewers appreciate confidence and power They do not appreciate arrogant or obnoxious people. Avoid believing that you are superior to everyone else, even though you think you are. Be honest about your achievements without boasting. Talk about your achievements without shouting about them. Be humble and show your strength with respect and respect. That is let your achievements and actions speak for themselves at the very least certain times.

Show your Passion!

Many people view an opportunity to work as a chance to earn more money or get the opportunity to take a week off. However, these motivations last only for a brief period of time. Once you get familiar with the higher pay and extra time off the actual issues of the job are likely to come up. This is something hiring managers and Human Resource people are well aware of.

What they are looking for from applicants is an enthusiasm for the position and the business. They're looking for applicants who have studied the company and understand what the job is like inside and out. They would like to hear what suggestions from applicants on how they can make things better and assist in helping the company expand.

They prefer people who think about the work first and then the pay check after that. The question of whether or not this is acceptable is up for debate but we should at least provide them with what they want and then sort the other issues in the future!

These are basic list of things to consider to remember when it's time for the interview. Let's shift gears for a moment and talk about the manner of conduct you must exhibit when you enter the room. Because attitude has every aspect to do presentation , and the interview itself is one big show with you at the center.

Here are some tips you need to consider in regards to the way you act and react in the course of your interview:

Make yourself a Solver

The job you're asked to interview for is a result of certain requirements and specific issues. It is essential to consider the way you approach this interview as the best problem solver in the world. You have to demonstrate to the interviewer and your company why you are capable to solve the problems they face.

There is a good chance that at some point you'll get a call from the director of the department that you will be working for. What better way to sit down with them than to explain to the manager that hiring you will help reduce the stress that comes on his desk each day. Imagine the impression you'd create when you tell the person why hiring your could help his job to be easier and less stress-inducing.

Do you have an easier method to convince people to work for you? I'm not sure.

Think like the Hiring Manager.

Similar to Be aware of who is conducting the interview and what their role is within the business. They usually provide this information when they introduce themselves. Make sure to address each answer to each question in the manner an individual in that position would like to listen to it. The answers should be as personal and relevant as they can be.

If you are interviewing the department's head in the near future respond to each question with the way you to make their department more efficient more productive, and more functioning. Let them know that a more efficient department means less stress for the supervisor.

Discuss each of your talents and achievements in a manner that makes clear what they can do to benefit your department and their company. Do not make generic statements, instead specifically targeted and specific assertions designed to impress your interviewer about their job.

Answering Questions

While having a relaxed attitude can be an advantage during interviews, it can result in problems. Be alert when you respond to questions, trying to answer them as fully as you can without being too rambling simultaneously. That is, give complete and thorough answers to each question, and then end your conversation. Do not engage in conversation and do not share personal stories, except to being friendly and pleasant towards the person interviewing you.

Many interviewers will ask questions that are designed to make you talk and share information that you normally would prefer to keep to yourself. Relax, but remain vigilant and cautious while you're at it. That's another reason you should practice your responses to the most frequently asked questions can help you to answer questions without having to provide more information.

Keep the message in mind

If you've completed your homeowner's job, you'll have a message or game plan to follow before you go to the interview. Make sure to stick to that strategy and plan, and don't give contradicting or contradicting signals. If you notice the original strategy evidently not working, stay focused and strive to get the conversation back where it was prior to.

If you begin with a specific focus only to alter it later in the course of the interview, the interviewer will be unsure if you're sincere or simply telling the truth about what they'd like to hear. Keep your focus focused, build your credibility, and ensure that your message and concentration throughout the interview.

Limit small Talk

You'd like to be friendly and not be distracted by small talk in the process. A professional and knowledgeable interviewer will be able to move the conversation in the right direction to make you divulge your personal information, or other information you would otherwise have kept secret. Keep conversation to a minimum, but be friendly and engaging while at the same time.

We've said it before avoid religion, politics and other controversial subjects and also off-color as well as ethnic variety. Sometimes, what you write and what you discuss can provide the most accurate picture of your personality. Be mindful before speaking and, if you have doubts, avoid it. It's better to stay more secure than uncertain.

Chapter 11: The Impression Factor

In the event that you have completed the preparations, there is another aspect that matters quite a bit. It is so important that I have decided to create an entire chapter on it . The other element is referred to as the "impression" aspect. It makes sense to a recruiter if you create a great impression before even opening your mouth. Your first impression could cast an impression on the rest the interview.

In this chapter , I'll give a more detailed description of what creates a positive impression on the person you are recruiting. Your impression can be described as a combination of the following

Dressing

The details of your dress should be precise.

Hairstyle, make-up, nails etc

Jewelry(if you wear one))

The accessories you keep

Arrived on time

Check in to your appointment

The recruiter's greeting and meeting

Body language

The way you begin the interview, then continue and end the interview

Dressing

Your appearance and appearance must signal to the recruiter that this day of your interview is special to you, not an ordinary day for business.

To stay safe both women and men are able to wear a more conservative formal business suit with a light colored shirt. Men can sport a bright tie, while women can embellish by wearing silk scarves (if they want). This is the usual formal and conservative business attire that no potential recruiter will be able to resist.

The reason I would like you to adopt the conservative approach when attire is that some recruiters are able to work to dress in any way insofar as it is compatible in line with the job you're applying for however, some recruiters are rigid and think formal attire is essential. So if you don't have an office space you can beg to borrow, borrow or even steel one of your sizes.

A general rule is that a business suite is essential for finance, accounting laws, taxation, and other desk-related occupations or jobs. If not, then it is the ultimate choice of the candidate being interviewed.

Details of your dress

The finer points of your attire are the thing that recruiters take a close examine. Some interviewees wearing identical dresses are equally dressed. I have interviewed interviewees who wear different specifics of dress, so be sure to take note of the following to see a more detailed description.

Your clothes are tidy, clean and stain-free

Your shirt is being pulled into

Your clothes are wrinkle-free and isn't stale.

Your tie is correctly tied and is positioned just beneath the button at the top on your shirt (little deviations are acceptable since it is the norm for all)

Nails, makeup, hair and jewellery

Your hair must be neat, clean and neatly haired. Makeup should not be excessively applied. Nails for men should be neat and the nails of women should be kept short enough to prevent the recruiter from asking "how do they use the keyboard". Make sure that jewelry is kept to a minimum, or avoid it altogether.

Belt and shoes

Take a close look at your belt and shoes. They're not the first items you'll need for an interview, but they are the clothes that form a large part of your first impression. When deciding on your shoe and belt, ensure that you follow the guidelines you have the following

Back and brown shades are the only options.

Black is by and is the most secure choice

Belt and shoes should be the same color.

They shouldn't be old or brand new.

You are at ease

Accessories

The accessories you wear are what you carry around with you. You should use the best quality of accessories. You should carry an excellent business notebook, preferably that matches the color of your belt and shoes or briefcases, a branded pen with a writing device, and an uncluttered handkerchief.

I remember a man who was carrying all these documents in a bag for shopping. A mistake like this can erase everything.

Arriving on time to the office

It is essential to be at the interview between 20 and 30 minutes prior to the interview time. This is because you will be able to take a look at the interview preparation templates within the last few minutes. It's not a problem arriving at least an hour early, so the condition is that you do not show up to the recruiter prior to 30 minutes before the time for interview because it appears that you're unemployed. Late arrivals will usually result in a straight rejection.

I have seen plenty of candidates who show up for interviews in a timely manner (we were used to calling them "J.I.T arriving candidates") but this leads to an extreme underperformance because applicants have a longer time to settle and relax. This is a major irritant to the fundamentals that the interviews are built on.

Be on time to your appointment

Once you are in the office you must first announce that you are arriving to reception. Don't underestimate the importance of this individual. The recruiters might seek their opinion on this person in addition to the fact that the moment you are chosen, you will work with the person. You must behave in a manner that is as gentle as you can.

While you wait, you can prepare yourself for the interview by using the templates for preparation. You may have a chat with the receptionist or with other interviewees. A journal or magazines can make a great impression. Avoid reading novel that is fiction because you're in the process of interviewing and need to look in a hurry, not relaxed.

You must ensure that you don't appear like a rat in the surveillance camera's view with your excessive movements. Also, go to the bathroom should it be needed(I suppose you've kept away from street food)

The first thirty second of the interview

One of the most effective methods to introduce yourself is to give an one-line introduction. You can start with "Hi I am ....and I am summoned for an interview with ...."Be more than willing for a hand shake but don't offer one and embarrass yourself if the recruiter doesn't return the hand shake for any reasons.

Based on the etiquettes following the etiquettes, you need to wait for the recruiter to give you seating. However , if the recruiter isn't able to offer you a seat for just a couple of seconds, be sure to sit in your own. The recruiter is not at any right to let you forget your how to behave.

Most likely, one of them can be proven to be true.

The person who is recruiting you wants to figure out how you respond if do not get an opportunity to sit in

The person who is recruiting them is too in the rush and loses track of the details.

Simply relax without thinking about it for a second.

Body language

The most important aspect in your conversation is the body language. I've observed that some people have excellent control of their tongue, but not their body language.

Many hiring managers are educated to spot even the smallest clues your body language gives to interpret the signals in the way they would like. It's not my intention to scare you. All I'm saying that you must present your body in a professional manner.

I would like you to know one aspect. It is important to prepare yourself before you imagine in the presentation of an appropriate body language. The best method to convey a professional physique is to learn as possible. Every time I've observed that those who have been well-prepared present an improved body language when compared to ones who are not prepared.

The message I would like to send to you is "you must take charge of your preparation and let the body language naturally take care of itself" The reason I'm saying that is because recruiters observe your body language in ways more subtle than you could imagine. Therefore, most of your efforts at fixing the body language and not address the causes of this body language will be in vain. In any case, if you're completed with your training and are looking to improve how you speak, recording some video clips from your practice interviews as well as then watching the results can be a great beginning.

Below are some of the emotions you're body language shouldn't be a reflection of.

Worry or fear

Anxiety

Desperation

A dispute by using your tongue

A few simple things you can perform to show your body in a more professional manner

Keep calm and calm.

Maintain eye contact

Sit straight and straight.

Don't cross your legs or with arms

Remain confident and shake hands when you are offered

Use any gadget in a manner that appears to be to be torturing

Do not look at the roof or one place over and over repeatedly.

The most important thing is to remember all I mentioned in the beginning i.e

The recruiter is looking for you.

You're good enough.

You have a 100 percent chances of being successful.

The interview is concluded.

Typically, the recruiter will ask "do there have you any concerns?" "No" is an extremely bad choice for the answer. There's a reason the question was posed in this manner. It is a reflection of your enthusiasm for the position. Ask questions. You may ask the recruiter for more specific in regards to the job's requirements, or you might want to inquire questions about recent press releases and forthcoming projects. This is logical.

You could even approach whether you are qualified for the role in an a respectful manner such as "based the conversation we had, I believe that I am the ideal candidate for this position. When do I expect to hear from you regarding the matter?" but refrain from explicit statements like "I would like to be considered for this position and when will I hear back?"

Exit

Leave the interview area like an ace. Display the same enthusiasm you display when you entered. Your recruiters are watching your exit. They can easily determine your thoughts about whether you'll be successful or fail by watching you leave.

Chapter 12: Bring Extra Copies To Interview

Always inquire if there's any specific item you have to bring to the interview. In addition to bringing your list of questions, it is recommended to bring copies of everything you will need to give for the interviewer, in the event that there multiple people taking part in the interview. Even if you're not required to bring references for the interview, make your time to write your answers and make copies. You will not be able to appear without the documents specifically requested by you. If you don't think that you will be able to obtain them within the time frame given, make certain to inform the interviewer that you are arriving to the interview.

Don't Be Late For The Interview

It is vital to never be late to an interview. There's no excuse for this (besides an incident or emergency in the family). Interviewers don't want to be told about being lost, causing traffic problems or losing track of time. They're taking time from their work to talk to you in order to offer you a job, so it's disrespectful and rude to not be punctual.

Here are some tips to prevent this from happening:

Perform a dry run If you are scheduled for an interview scheduled in the city or in a region of the city you're not familiar with, then, take tests to measure the time it takes to drive.

Leave Early: Get up early enough so that you can get to the building 30-60 minutes prior to your scheduled interview time. Don't enter the building, instead find the nearest coffee shop and sit down.

Pay for parking: Do not walk around the block in search of inexpensive parking in the streets. Make a payment for parking in a garage parking lot and create unnecessary stress.

Therefore, if you're running behind, be sure to contact. The interviewer might have other priorities and not be able to finish the interview. I hope the interviewer is understanding and allow you to make another appointment as soon as possible.

Be Confident In The Interview

Even the most confident candidate can be nervous in a job interview. However, you need to project confidence.

Always keep eye contact. There is nothing more a obvious sign of a lack of confidence in yourself than someone who doesn't glance at someone in the eye. Begin by walking up to the interviewer, shake their hand, and look the direction of their eyes as you greet them . You should also acknowledge your joy at getting to know them. Remember that you were granted the interview because of your qualifications So, use this information to build and increase your confidence. Your confidence will grow with time as you participate in more interviews.

Be honest in the Interview

Always be honest and do not lie in an interview to make you appear more impressive than you really are. Don't divulge information that can't be confirmed by your former or current employer or by the references you supply. Inadvertently revealing your educational background is a great chance to be in problems, therefore if you do not possess a degree, don't claim to possess one. Make sure to highlight your positive qualities when you are interviewed. If you were involved in a project, tell the interviewer about the role that you took on and the way you contributed to the overall achievement that the initiative. Being honest will always place you in the most favorable image.

Be precise when answering interview questions

Even if you're a bit nervous during an interview, you should pay attention and focus on the interviewer's question before you respond. If an interviewer says they're looking for a specific answer be sure to not provide an unspecific answer because this is a surefire way of damaging your chances of getting the job. These kinds of questions are called situationsal questions. If you were asked by an interviewer that to you "Tell us about your favourite vacation spot." You shouldn't answer by describing every city you'd prefer to visit, or even make an generalization. Employers want to know your response or performance in particular circumstances.

The most frequently asked questions are:

"Tell me about a specific moment in your life when you were the leader of the team for a project." In the description, tell me the details of the project and how many people were involved you had to manage, and any difficulties you encountered and how you dealt with these.

"Tell me of a dispute that you and a coworker had." Choose only scenarios that resulted in positive outcomes.

Employers are now looking to find out what you will do on the job before they decide to employ you. When you answer questions that are specific to the situation, you will be able to show the interviewer that you possess the abilities and thinking processes they're searching for. Be precise but concise It is possible that you are someone who talks wildly when they're stressed or who clams into a stressful situation It is important to be aware of this and refrain from doing the same during an interview. Interviewers want enough details to help them comprehend the subject matter you're discussing without wasting time with irrelevant details.

Be careful not to use terminology or acronyms when presenting examples from your past or current job. Use common phrases that the majority of the population is acquainted with. When discussing projects, describe what the project involved including the number of people involved and how you managed the project. The interviewer isn't likely want to hear a complete play by performance of the entire process and they're interested in knowing your part in the project. Make sure you stay on topic and don't get distracted and forget what idea you wanted to convey. It's an excellent idea practicing with a buddy or family member prior to your interview.

How to Answer The Hard Interview Questions

Every interview will have at the very least one question you aren't sure of what the right answer is. It's the one you think about for days, and then go over and through it over and over in your mind and ask other interviewers which answers they would have given. It is impossible to avoid these kinds of questions, but you are able to respond to confidently to keep your mind at ease until you hear back.

Don't feel like you must answer immediately when you are asked an question. There is no TV show where the contestant with the fastest time to answer the question wins. The interviewers will appreciate the fact the fact that you took time to think about and plan your answer. If you're concerned about an extended silence, don't be- it's normal. If you've been asked a question and you aren't sure how to respond, take to take a few moments to think of a suitable answer. It is better than having to take a long time to reply without explaining what you're doing.

If you're unable to think of an answer in a hurry, ask if it is possible to return to the question in a minute keep trying to come up with an answer. Don't believe that if reach the end of your interview and haven't responded to the question, you're out of the loop. If your interviewer does not ask for another the question, it isn't without being noticed that you did not respond to an inquiry. The best scenario is to bring the subject back to the question and respond the question in a way that is appropriate. Thanks to your interviewer for giving you extra time to think of the correct answer. If it's a long question that has been broken down into smaller pieces cut it into smaller pieces, and don't attempt to solve it all in one go It is always possible to request sections that are asked to repeat.

Silences and Pauses Throughout The Interview

There will be instances during an interview where there are pauses in conversations or total silence. This could be initiated by you or by the interviewer, and usually it isn't a sign of something wrong. It is possible to take a minute to think of a solution and in the meantime there's likely to be a complete silence. This is perfectly normal. Do not be distracted by the fact that no one is talking. Use the time you've been given to find the most effective solution or example you can provide. If you are interviewing with a notepad (and the odds are that they will be) take your time and be at ease with the fact that there are going to there will be pauses between the questions as they try to record everything. This can be a positive factor because it signifies that they are impressed by your answers and are likely to recall it in the future when they make the decision they will hire.

If you've responded to an inquiry and are answered with silence, and the interviewer isn't doing anything or completing the interview, you could be confused on what to do. It could mean that the interviewer is looking for more details or that they are not happy with your answer. You'll never know until you ask "Do you wish to go into more detail?" If the answer is no, simply sit back and wait until the following question is asked. Do not worry about the fact that the interviewer isn't giving you praise for the answer to every question before moving on to the next. They don't want to provide you with an idea of your performance during the interview . They're trained to remain neutral when responding to questions even if they don't respond at all.

Chapter 13: Experiences and Experiences

We'll walk you through your resume

Effectively respond to the interview. Make sure you focus on the sections of your resume which will let you demonstrate that you are the most suitable candidate to do the job. Learn to give a more precise response in between 2 and three minutes.

The interviewer should be able to talk about your professional experience. Start by describing your two most recent posts. Highlight the abilities that are relevant to the position you're applying. Additionally, If you're from a different sector write down the reasons that have led you to change careers. You should also identify the skills that could be required in both sectors.

The most important thing is to highlight the abilities that are relevant to the position you're applying for , and then provide specific examples and details.

The winning answer:

As you'll see on my resume, I work by ABC Title Company as an Escrow Officer. In my position I am responsible for overseeing the real estate sales, purchases and refinances. As an Escrow Officer I review the files and balance them as well as review the title documentation and make sure that everyone is in line with the costs, and also visit with the lenders as well as the home buyers to clarify all information regarding the title documents, fees, and documentation.

Prior to my current job I worked as an agent for real estate in my previous city. We had to relocate due to commitments to family and I did not have the same networks I had in my previous residence, which is why I switched to escrow work. I was a top-producing agent at Jenky Realty, and I focused on multi-million-dollar sales.

The two roles, though distinct from the job of loan originator I'm seeking, work in the same field. I am now a part of a strong network and, with my expertise in every aspect of the home-buying process, I can become an outstanding loan originator.

Do you want me to review my CV and my experience?

What do you think your former superiors would have to say about You?

Don't wait until the interview to learn what the response to that question is. Do your research and inquire with your current or past bosses to provide feedback about your performance in the workplace as soon as you are able. Make sure you solicit an affirmative reference through an official letter of recommendation in the event that it is it is possible. This will help you provide a truthful answer. Write your letter of recommendation confidently. It will make a great impression on the manager who is hiring you as you're well-prepared and are showing determination.

Answer that is winning:

I have an endorsement letter here and you can read it right from where it came from. I'm certain that, should you speak to him, you'd find that I was a valuable important asset to his company. He would often tell me that I was appreciated for my hard work and dedication to completing the task correctly. We enjoyed a great relationship and I'll be sad to part ways with him, however, he was able to help me become ready for the job.

Take us through a typical Day from Your Most Recent position

Interviewers may be asking you this question in order to learn about your job duties and similarities to the job that you're applying for. It's easy to answer, just be sure to give a straight answer. You should highlight specific areas of your day-to-day work schedule to demonstrate to your interviewer how efficient and motivated you are and in particular, in the areas that are most relevant to the position that you've applied for.

You should provide enough information about your work day routine however, don't give a minute-by-minute blow-by-blow account of everything you're doing every day. Focus on what's practical or real instead of "ideal" circumstances and make sure you say not to criticize your coworkers. Also, make sure to mention the challenges that you have overcome regularly and are success. Highlight your personal efficiency and ability to tackle the challenges of work.

A Winner's Answer

I don't work on a typical time. My schedule is "scheduled" for work from from 8 to 5, however, I've made a commitment to myself to complete my work until it is completed. I typically arrive at the office around 7 am. This lets me avoid congestion, and also allows me to finish certain routine emails and operational requirements. Since people typically arrive at the office around 8am, I have a clear idea of my schedule and priorities. I usually set at minimum one goal that is unalterable, which means that I'll not leave my office until I've achieved the goal I've established for myself. The reason I do this is by reading The Seinfeld Book, "Don't Break the Chain." As I mentioned I make sure to address emails and other operational issues and prioritize my work from 7:15 to 8:30. In the morning, we hold a the daily sales meeting which is where we talk about all new items or requirements. 8:30-9:00, I review the clients that are on the list of clients to call the day before and ensure I have their records in order and that the work required to be completed has been completed. If there's any follow-up work to be completed, I present it before the service team to ensure that everything is up to date. Between 9:00 and 11:00, I make my first period of prospecting. I have found that clients are the most open in the morning, and in later in the afternoon. When I am 11:15, I go through any emails or voicemails that are received and immediately respond to any urgent needs. In the afternoon, I eat some food. .... I typically bring my food so that I can check my email at work and catch up. From 12:30 to 3.30, I generally set up appointments for clients. The time between 3:30 and 4:00 is a catch-up while 4:00-6:00 is an additional outside call blocking. Between 6:00 and 6:30, I typically review my schedule to see if I've met my objectives for the day, and then plan for the following day.

That's what I'm constantly striving to accomplish during my working day, however frequently things go off track. Although I might not adhere to this plan due to demands from clients or appointments that are longer or training, or even unexpected meetings This is my routine when I'm not distracted.

I'm more successful using this method when I plan my monthly, quarterly, annual and weekly goal-setting. It helps me prioritize my tasks for me. I do not let a day pass without making a prospect. Making sure that my pipeline is full is my first priority.

Discuss a difficult work situation and the Way You Overcame It. Surmont It

If you are asked to answer the question, be aware that the majority of job interviewers are looking to find out how you can deal with or solve a problem. Make sure to highlight the aspects of these situations which show your capacity to solve problems. By answering this question, you'll be able to show your capacity to take charge and maybe, your coaching ability when a situation is beyond your control.

Pay attention to any of the following important aspects when you answer the answer:

A challenging situation for which you have found a solution, and how you achieved it;

A moral situation in which you choose the integrity over compromise

Examples of situations where you tackled the possibility of or dealt with a challenging issue;

The situations where you have acknowledged your weaknesses and actively asked for help from your superiors in resolving a problem.

Like the other questions, anticipating is crucial. You must prepare your answer to this question ahead of time as you'll be unable to come up with a convincing answer just by musing on the spot. Make sure you organize your thoughts so that you are able to answer the question clearly.

Beware of being blamed. If there is some truth in the story of someone else who created the problem this will reflect poorly to you, if you present the story from this angle. It can appear as if you're trying to justify your actions or not accepting responsibility.

It's acceptable to be a victim and be blamed for a challenging circumstance.

Make sure to clarify your motives to become a better or more effective employee. Share your lessons learned.

Do not paint yourself as an expert in dealing with difficult or challenging situations. Be sure to convey your message in a straightforward manner. The arrogance of a person can cause for concern.

The winning answer:

Our customer service team was given a mandate to alter the way we interact with customers through the inclusion of a questionnaire tool in our conversations. We already had high expectations. The company was one of the top clients in the country in terms of satisfaction. However, the introduction of the tool made it more difficult to maintain a smooth dialogue with customers. In the middle of a conversation, the client could lose interest and become disengaged. In the end, staff members in customer service ignored the rules. They'd be compensated based for the total engagement with clients but they were not willing to sacrifice their bonuses.

I spoke to the manager of the project in order to learn why the management team demanded that we include this tool into the discussions. It appears that at other firms using this tool, results demonstrated that upon the use by this instrument, the conversion sales rates doubled. With a greater grasp of "why," I committed myself to becoming an expert in the subject area of the tool. If it was able to triple sales conversions, then I wanted to be part of it. After a few months and some training, I was more adept than the majority of people making use of the tool. I reached a point where I still had high customer satisfaction ratings and experienced more use of the tool than any other person in the company. After I proved to myself that this could be done, I spoke with the management team about my challenges and what I had to do to change my negative attitude and shared my step-by-step process to become proficient. I suggested that we communicate my method with the rest of the country and they embraced the idea. When they introduced their brand new "training" and provided more details about what they call the "why," the adoption of the new tool increased from 30% to 90 percent. Based on my ideas, I received an award for partnership and innovation.

Let us know about a time You disagreed with a Company Initiative

This is a difficult issue to address. Interviewers recognize that humans aren't perfect and there will be instances that people don't agree with decisions made by the leadership. Be sure to provide a real answer that does not create the impression that you're insubordinate. Keep in mind that the interviewer is seeking to know more about your diplomatic skills and ability to cope with conflicts. Keep to the facts and don't be emotionally involved. It's essential to be ready to make concessions if circumstances don't go in the direction you'd like.

Answer that is winning:

I've always believed it's essential to pick your fights. If it's appropriate I am a firm believer in being respectfully disagreeing and standing my position, and always contemplating the best interests of the whole group. Recently I found myself in a position in which I needed to utilize this method of thought to express my thoughts regarding an issue that I was not happy with the direction taken by the company.

As a supervisor of a sales team I've always believed that the greatest advantage is selecting the best people. If you choose to hire the top employees, and have a solid process in place and you're a great coach, the results will follow. However, the management team from the top was feeling that sales managers weren't performing the tasks they were required to do and so they chose to limit themselves by the lowest common factor.

They set up specific tasks like the amount of meetings, calls and so on. to be held. They wanted to increase the purpose by controlling aggressively to meet the goals.

The way they chose to tackle this issue did not match my belief that top salespeople "shine" when they are allowed to do what they are good at. Highly successful salespeople are not happy being given a specific instruction on what they should do. After hearing the feedback of several salespeople, I spoke to my boss in a respectful manner and explained my concerns. She was extremely and open to discussion. She was in the same boat and shared the same concerns. Talking about it helped me feel better however, it was a shame that it was not a fight between us that we could influence. She was willing to discuss concerns, but then guided me on the causes and ways to support my team. You won't be able to win every battle however it does make the difference to talk about your issues and not be accused of it. It's equally important to don the "corporate" dress when required and reinforce the message whenever appropriate.

What is the most difficult or best job You've Had?

The question, while appearing easy to answer, is actually one that the interviewer is trying to discover subtle aspects about your personality and character more than just the job you enjoyed or disliked. It's likely to be more about "why" of your choice of the best or worst job offers.

To get the best job, you should choose the ones which allow you to use your abilities or strengths and, if it is possible you can choose jobs that are relevant to the position for which you're applying.

Winning answer for best job:

I enjoyed working for Smith Industries. It was a challenging job and I gained lots. I also learned be able to speak in an entirely different way with the management team. Smith Industries valued feedback at all levels. You can be a positive influence when you put yourself on the market. It wasn't the most enjoyable job I've ever held but I was happy to be an integral part of the solution.

Answers to the most awful job you've ever worked at will reveal some of your character traits that are negative Take consideration when deciding on your answer, and especially the "why" to back it up. Select the "worst" jobs in which the motive behind choosing this job can be described as"positive negative. "positive negativity."

A winning solution for the most difficult job:

When I was working for Jones Corporation, there was constantly pressure to be against my own ethics of integrity and honesty. For instance... for as it wasn't "explicitly" made it was felt that there was a chance to extend the limits. I realized that every person has their own ethical line and mine was clearly defined.

If the intent of the law is to establish boundaries around one aspect, I will abide to the law's spirit. This is an instance of when my ethics were challenged ....

OR an alternative Winning solution to the most difficult job:

I enjoyed working at Jones Corp because of the immense amount of knowledge I acquired. It was then clear that it wasn't a good match for me since it took me so long without my loved ones, and forced me to miss my children's development.

The interviewer can understand the problem with the job or that it wasn't due to a persona or cultural fit. Similar to the previous examples avoid negative remarks about the former employer or the individuals.

Chapter 14: What are Your Three Most Significant Weaknesses?

Variants of the Question

What is your biggest weakness?

Guide

This is an untruthful question. On one the other hand, if your answer is too transparent, you'll frighten the interviewer and won't get the job. However you must create an answer that is professional and addresses the weaknesses you have.

There are many methods to tackle this. My preferred method is to choose an area of weakness that is an opportunity to disguise a strength. It's easy to think of these as you consider your strengths. Here are a few examples (the weak point precedes the strength by using parentheses):

I'm generally slow (because I'm meticulous and always do high-quality work).

I am a person-pleaser (which means that I am easy and enjoyable to be around).

I am prone to being slightly self-confident (because I'm confident in my abilities and sell lots).

I'm not the most effective listener (because I'm clever and have usually the most innovative ideas).

I make mistakes from time to time (because I'm fast and love to finish my work before deadlines).

Although, some sound awful. If you spin them correctly they can be great and turn you into an appealing potential candidate.

After you've picked two weak points, you must form your answer. In general you should structure your answer into two parts. The first one is a short description of your weaknesses while the second is your approach to the issue. It is important to turn everything into a positiveand stimulating answer. Keep in mind that every flaw is an opportunity to grow - you only need to communicate your message in the interview. It is possible to be asked to speak about one weakness, however it is always advisable to be prepared with a few. There are two examples below. They can help you set up for a fantastic answer.

Examples of Bullets

One weakness: I tend to get bogged down in the finer details and cover the entire gamut.

The weakness: When given an assignment, I attempt to ensure that every space is taken care of, but sometimes , this slows me down.

Secret Strengths: My positive side is that I consistently offer high-quality work.

Solution: I've taught me to pull myself back every 10 mins to consider whether the activity I was doing was serving the bigger objective.

My weakness 2: I am a person-pleaser. I am prone to doing things I don't prefer to do in order to please people.

A weakness I tend towards wanting people love me, which is why I strive to be nice to them.

Undiscovered Strength: One positive aspect lies in the fact that I'm likable and easy to collaborate with. People love working with me.

Solution: Before I answer "yes" to anyone else I began to consider if this is the right thing to do now to finish the task.

Have you ever failed in anything? Variants

I would like to hear about a moment that you did not do effectively.

Let me know about a difficult scenario you encountered and you failed to achieve success.

Guide

In this case, the interviewer would like to know the fact that even when you don't succeed in something, you can learn how to improve your performance the next time. Employers today tend to emphasize that if you fail, you won't fail. To be successful, you have to demonstrate resilience, the ability to fail but bounce back. It doesn't have to be a result of work.

Examples of Bullets

Situation: I was looking to join a particular student group to learn more about my future job.

Action: I applied but did not get into. I sought feedback on my application from everyone I could.

The result: I learned to write excellent applications. I also became a teacher and assisted others in their careers.

Example Answer

When I was in college, I was looking to be a part of InSite. InSite was a fellowship program that offered services for consulting to startups at the beginning of their journey. I was interested because it was an awesome experience to help others create something from scratch. We were required to write an official cover letter (since I didn't grow up in the States I was unsure what it means). We were also required to compose a brief case analysis. I remember juggling all of my schoolwork and other activities to make sure I did the right answer. I did research on companies for a case study to write about and then I stayed up until late to create an intriguing case study. I also had other people review the cover letters. I was eager to submit all of my documents within the deadline. But, unfortunately, I wasn't accepted.

This was a fantastic opportunity. I was unable to attend, which meant I missed my sole chance to get into. I was devastated. My first reaction was to think "screw the thing" and move forward. But, I did something entirely different. I presented myself to one the InSite members, and had her discuss ways to enhance my resume. She was able to review many of my cover letters and resumes as I began applying for jobs. Overall although I didn't make it through I learned the most of this learning experience. I learned how to create resumes, applications, and cover letters. I also turned it into an additional business!

Let me know your work routine

Question Variants

Please tell me something about what you are doing in your present job

What would you say about your job?

Guide

This might seem like something that is easy to answer however when you ask it you have to take a long time to find an appropriate answer. The majority of people simply explain the things they do in their position. This isn't the best method. Actually, this question could be another chance to show off your accomplishments. In order to provide an engaging answer, we're looking to write mini-stories in bullet points. Examples include:

Management of people to demonstrate leadership and management abilities.

The project will show you are able to comprehend the bigger picture and interact with different kinds of people.

Use software to show that you have the technical and analytical abilities.

Anything that shows your problem-solving abilities.

Below are some examples of the qualities. Below each example is an example of how to demonstrate it in a specific job. The format of the solution should read:

A short description of your work.

3 to 6 sentences about the abilities you'd like to emphasize.

A closing sentence that offers an extra something an indication of that you have gone over and above.

Exemple Bullets with Stories

Technical abilities I'm responsible for the management of the network at our office. I am part of a team consisting of two individuals who manage around 500 stations. We use an automated ticketing system and in a typical day I can handle between 30 and 80 tickets. My main objective is to ensure that the system is always in operation and that everyone is content and productive. For me, if someone is waiting around for something I am unable to fix, I've failed at my job.

Analytical abilities: I work often using Excel and creating complicated models. These models aid management in understanding the issues and strategic challenges that the company faces. They provide management with a clear picture of the situation that can help them decide about the best direction to take. Beyond my analytical capabilities I also make proposals based on my personal opinions. Sometimes, management has taken my suggestions into their corporate strategy.

Management skills Sales management skills: As a sales manager, I manage a team of five that report to me. I view my role as making sure my team is equipped with everything it requires to be successful. I'm always available to assist them when they require my assistance. I believe in hands-off leadership and let my team go until they encounter an obstruction. It's equally important to ensure that my team members are happy with the amount of work I assign them. I attempt to split the accounts in accordance with my understanding regarding the capabilities of my team members. This way, we can all to move the company forward with our top abilities.

Skills to solve problems Skills for customer support: As a representative, I earned an average score 9.0 9.5 out of hundreds customers. I achieved this by asking the right questions to pinpoint the root cause of the problem. If the answer wasn't immediately clear I then contacted my colleagues for assistance. After gathering all the relevant information in this manner I was able help a lot of customers.

People skills: At my previous job, I set up an organization called a movie club. The group got monthly to watch movies. My coworkers were enthusiastic about the idea and there was great participation. Then we got a grant from management to take us to the cinema and make it an annual corporate celebration. This helped us boost our culture as well as the employee morale.

Skills in organization: I have an organizational system that is based on the book "Getting Things done." I write down all my tasks into Evernote and label them with who, what and where as well as when. This has helped me manage my time and also change priorities quickly. This is crucial since deadlines are constantly changing frequently. This has helped me stay focused on finishing my task in time and submit it in high-quality.

Management skills for project management as a product manager I was responsible for numerous features in our product. I was part of a multi-functional global team. I was responsible for coordinating meetings across time zones. I also set objectives, success criteria as well as the procedures to meet these goals. I made sure that everyone was meeting deadlines and that projects were moving forward.

Ability to lead The time we experienced massive layoffs at the workplace my group of five was reduced to three and there was plenty of work to be done. Morale was down due to reductions. I wanted to ensure my employees remained focussed and focused. I did a few things. First, I held an all-team meeting to inform everyone about what was happening and listen to their concerns. Then , I held one-on-one meetings so that everyone could discuss their concerns. I urged everyone to remain focus and not shy away from the responsibility. I explained that tough moments are the most beneficial to learn and gain experience. We learned how to handle the circumstances. All went well and we were able to complete tasks in time. Then we expanded to become a bigger team than we were before.

Creativity As an engineer for an music software company, I created a three-part class for engineers to learn how to play the drums. Additionally, I taught the engineers to read the rhythm notes. This allowed them to better understand the requirements of our customers. Through this innovative idea I was able to benefit the business. I was able combine my love of music and the development of software to accomplish this.

Chapter 15: Identifying Potential Interviewees

Overview

Contacting potential interviewees is a simple but time-consuming process. It's an crucial step as you'll need to identify those who you believe can assist you in achieving your goals and then reaching out to the person to obtain their consent to conduct an informational interview. The process of identifying potential interviewees is not an easy task, however it may require some research to locate the contact details for people you want to talk to. I would suggest using the following websites to find persons to talk with:

1. Theorganization's site

2. Google

3. LinkedIn

Prospective Interviewee Prospective Interviewee Strategies

Organization Website: At this point, you should already have identified the numerous companies that are associated with your field of importance. If, for instance, you work in accounting, you'll need a an inventory of around 10-20 companies that you intend to study. You should have also researched specific positions that are of interest to you within those companies. When you visit any organizational website, your goal is to concentrate on the departments where your work of interest are situated. Keep track of names or contact information. Another benefit of finding names of interviewees you are considering by this method is that you may conduct informational interviews with individuals who are employed in the department that your job of interest are. It's not difficult to determine the possibility that the person you interview could assist you in securing one of the positions you've applied for, especially when they are connected to the department, for example, having contacts with the hiring manager of the job.

Google

While you browse through corporate websites, keep a search for people with their official titles and email addresses posted. Persons who are open (or at least wish to appear as being open) to receiving messages by email typically have their email address listed somewhere on the site alongside their name. Even if a number is given make sure you do not contact them. This is due to the fact that cold-calling for an informational interview is seen as unprofessional and is extremely rude. In the end, the reason you search for people who have names is that it provides you with a picture of their role within the company and depending on the position they hold you might be able find out more details about their background. For instance, they might have a personal biography that goes to their name, as common among executives. When you've found an individual of interest, you can search their name to determine if there's additional information available about the person. Apart from searching just the name of someone, you can consider using their name combination with the company or other company they might be associated with or were previously connected to. The goal is to collect as much information as you can. The information you collect can help provide context information about the person they are and what they do. This can be useful when you are preparing the interview questions, the letter of introduction, or when you conduct your informational interview.

Google The Google search engine is one of the best methods of identifying potential interviewees is to use to use the Google Search engine. It is important to consider the terms or concepts that relate to your potential interviewee in particular, or your field generally. For instance, if you were fascinated by fashion and were looking to find potential interviewees from Vogue Magazine You could use the search block to find "list of the people working in Vogue". Of course, you'll require to alter your search term in order to get your desired outcomes. I've actually tested it on my own and typed into the search box "Vogue Staff list for Vogue magazine" and got astonishing results. The search results showed the names of those who work at Vogue that included Anna Wintour, along with each editor of the magazine. Though I was unable to find their contact details, it could have be the matter of digging further on the site, or just searching for them in their own individual. Imagine being able to be able to get an interview with one of the fashion editors who could provide an invaluable career guidance or even an opportunity simply because you're in the perfect spot at the appropriate moment!

The advantage of making use of Google and other popular search engines this way is that it typically produce results that cascade. If, for instance, you search for someone's name, you'll usually find individuals associated with the person who could be equally qualified to be your interviewer. While you might have been searching for a specific individual related to their current position it is possible to discover a plethora of others with similar backgrounds , which could be a good source for an informational interview. The process of identifying people should not be a daunting partsince you'll be able to easily find a vast array of potential interviewees. It is more important to narrow the list to a manageable amount of applicants to talk with. Remember that it's a numbers game. It is unlikely that everyone you contact will respond positively in any way. This is why you must make an effort to find the maximum number of people you can and then focusing -- to maximum extent--on the character of the potential interviewee.

LinkedIn If you're not familiar with LinkedIn it's the largest professional social network in the world (I have this information because it is stated on their site). Professionals from across the globe can create profiles and interact with fellow professionals at the touch of one button. LinkedIn lets you create an online model of your CV. I can assure you that I have met a many professionals who aren't connected to LinkedIn. If you don't have an account on LinkedIn account, I'd suggest you start one now because you're not using one of the best methods of connecting with fellow professionals. It doesn't matter how you're old, whether you're at the end of your high school years or near to retirement. If you are professional (or at a minimum, an potential professional) then you must have an LinkedIn account. Period.

> Never ask a prospective interviewee or hiring official the answers to questions you can easily find on the company's website.

Let's discuss how you can make use of LinkedIn to locate potential interviewees. When you sign-up for your account on LinkedIn, you fill it with all kinds of personal information including professional and personal. LinkedIn utilizes the information you provide to connect you to people who have a lot in common with you, either in part or in total. For instance, if are currently enrolled in, or have attended University of Maryland, or graduated from the University of Maryland, LinkedIn could display a list of individuals who attended the university this could be a large number, in fact. If you want to target those with whom you have something in common, you could just conduct a search. Let's say, for instance, you're the same person looking for fashion, and you want to find out who from Vogue Magazine attended your alma school which is which is the University of Maryland. Simply enter that criteria into the search engine to ensure that it can perform the cross-reference.

After you have received your results, then you'll be able to make an email to them asking them to include you on their database of connections. You are free to connect with whomever you like. But there are a few points to keep in mind. In the first place, based on your profile the person you ask to connect with will not agree to your request. If your credentials aren't on the same level, or if they are not familiar with them, they won't be able to accept your request. But, don't be discouraged by this. Your task is to concentrate on creating a solid profile and then connecting with anyone you'd like to.

The majority of people tend to connect with people with whom they have in common with their professional interests for instance, if they are in the same field of work. However, this being stated, if you sign up to upgrade your access you will be able to send a set number of personal messages along with your request, instead of just the generic"request for connection" message that is included with access for free. The more specific your message is, the more likely they are to be willing to connect. Even if you have access for free Try to connect with others in your profession, industry or a company that you are interested in.

If someone is willing to accept the request you made, then are able to then send them as many messages as you like. I suggest sending the person a brief message explaining why you are connected to them and why you'd like to conduct an interview. Sometimes , people respond, but some do not. If they don't respond don't consider it a personal attack. But, there's an extremely good chance that people will reply positively. Furthermore, when they connect with you via LinkedIn most likely, they'll include their email in their profile. This is where you can send them a more specific message.

When you conduct your informal interviews, ask the interviewee if or she is interested in connecting to you on LinkedIn. This is how you can grow your professional network, by making connections with other people. From all platforms I believe LinkedIn to be more than just the most simple and efficient however, it is also the most advanced. The trick is to build the LinkedIn profile with the same diligence and attention to detail that you'd add to your resume. Be aware that potential employers will be able to view your profile, which a majority of people do before they decide to accept an invitation to join. Be certain to conduct a thorough study of LinkedIn manners of conduct to not only adhere to acceptable standards of conduct however, to avoid any dangers.

How do you contact prospective interviewees?

After you have created an outline of the people you would like to interview, you'll need to reach them in order to obtain their consent to hold the meeting. Contrary to what may seem to be the most rational strategy, don't simply pick up the phone and make a call. The method you use to reach them is through a formal letter of introduction you send to them (discussed in the next chapter). The only reason you should actually contact a prospective interviewee is when someone has given permission to talk to the person you are interviewing directly, for example, gatekeepers. A quick note for those who aren't familiar to the concept of gatekeeper, it's those who control access to other people.

The reason you should not contact an interviewee you might be interested in by yourself is that it is an actual cold-call. A "cold-call" is when someone who you don't know contacts you and asks for an inquiry from you. One way to ensure a swing and missed call is to contact someone who is working and ask for the opportunity to conduct an interview. People are inclined to take in requests similar to this one and then respond in a manner that suits them. The idea of putting the person you are interviewing on the spot at work is invasive and is likely to result in a negative outcome for you. A note of introduction can be a simple method of establishing contact with someone and request permission to conduct an interview.

In terms of the kind of people that you should contact all are fair game from the CEO down to rank and file staff. The higher up in the food chain you aim for the more influence they will have but the less likely you will receive an answer, especially in large corporations. But, you could succeed in getting in touch with C-level (or C-suite)executives and executives, especially those who work for smaller boutique firms. C-level executives are those with a titles start with"Chief" that is, for example, chief executive officer or Chief information officer. If you decide to concentrate solely on senior executives, acceptable, but keep in mind that staff at mid-levels can be extremely beneficial to your cause too. Apart from their accessibility general to mid-level employees might also be more inclined to lend their time. In the end you've got no risk and gain from focusing on anyone of any rank. The most likely scenario is that they either will not respond or inform you that they are not available. Also, don't ignore people might be competent enough to give useful career guidance. Be aware that information is the most valuable asset today.

Conclusion

If you've completed the guidelines in this guide, you are fully prepared to find the job you've always wanted. Keep in mind that finding work and being hired is not an straightforward job. It requires dedication and determination.

Keep in mind that not many people find the job you apply to. It is not advisable to place all your eggs into one basket, as it were. Apply to a variety of jobs each day, instead of putting all your hopes and dreams on one particular job. If you're lucky, you'll get interviews, and then be offered various positions. You will be able to choose your choice, and with the additional benefit of earning the salary you desire (within the limits of).

Each time you take an interview, you'll become more confident in the procedure. Sometimes , it takes many interviews before they're fully confident and at ease. It is likely that you'll have to be undergoing multiple interviews for different positions with many companies before being actually offered a job. This is fine. It is rare for anyone to get an employment offer on the first attempt.

www.ingramcontent.com/pod-product-compliance
Lightning Source LLC
Chambersburg PA
CBHW071833080526
44589CB00012B/1037